Have Talent, Will Travel:
Directory of Authors, Illustrators, and Storytellers East of the Mississippi

By Gwynne Spencer

Linworth Publishing, Inc.
Worthington, Ohio

For Elly and Ruth.

Library of Congress Cataloging-in Publication Data

Spencer, Gwynne.
  Have talent, will travel : directory of authors, illustrators, and storytellers east of the Mississippi / by Gwynne Spencer.
     p. cm.
Includes indexes.
  ISBN 1-58683-050-3 (perfect bound)
  1. Children's libraries--Activity programs--United States. 2. School libraries--Activity programs--United States. 3. Children--Books and reading--United States. 4. Reading promotion--United States. 5. Authors, American--East (U.S.)--Directories. 6. Storytellers--East (U.S.)--Directories. 7. Illustrators--East (U.S.)--Directories.
I. Title.
Z718.2.U6 S678 2003
027.62'51'02578--dc21
                                             2003040016

Published by Linworth Publishing, Inc.
480 East Wilson Bridge Road, Suite L
Worthington, Ohio 43085

Copyright © 2002 by Linworth Publishing, Inc.

All rights reserved. Purchasing this book entitles a librarian to reproduce activity sheets for use in the library within a school or entitles a teacher to reproduce activity sheets for single classroom use within a school. Other portions of the book (up to 15 pages) may be copied for staff development purposes within a single school. Standard citation information should appear on each page. The reproduction of any part of this book for an entire school or school system or for commercial use is strictly prohibited. No part of this book may be electronically reproduced, transmitted, or recorded without written permission from the publisher.

ISBN 1-58683-050-3

5 4 3 2 1

Table of Contents

Acknowledgments iii
Introduction v
Tips on Arranging Your Event 1
Alabama 11
Connecticut 13
Delaware 19
Florida 21
Georgia 29
Illinois 33
Indiana 41
Kentucky 43
Maine 45
Maryland 49
Massachusetts 53
Michigan 63
Mississippi 69
New Hampshire 71
New Jersey 75
New York 83
North Carolina 109
Ohio 111
Pennsylvania 115
Rhode Island 121
South Carolina 125
Tennessee 127
Vermont 129
Virginia 131
Washington, D.C. 137
West Virginia 139
Wisconsin 141
Resources: Cyber and Others 147
Index by Performer 149
Index by State 153
About the Author 157

Acknowledgments

My heartiest thanks for making this book possible go to Betty Morris, JoEllen Misakian, and all the folks at Linworth who held steady through the many changes. Without the unflagging help of everyone at the Mancos Post Office, the manuscript might not have made it to the finish line. Without the encouragement of all the Cosmic Raccoons, I would have lost hope. In the course of the writing, I've learned from them all that it's not enough to make the world a better place just once in your lifetime—you have to do it every day.

Gwynne Spencer
Mancos, Colorado
2003

Introduction

The challenge facing those of us who love books and reading is simple: How do we make reading fashionable for kids? In a world filled with "virtual" everything, live storytelling, live presentations, and meeting celebrities still have the power to make the heart sing. When we connect kids with authors, storytellers, and illustrators, we make it safe for them to love reading and fashionable for them to love books.

Before the days of "www.com" there were only a few ways to find real, live authors and illustrators and storytellers, and one of those was to ask the local friendly bookseller if they knew any local talent.

One day at my children's bookstore, trespassers william in Albuquerque, I got a phone call requesting contact information for Joe Hayes, New Mexico's premier storyteller. I couldn't help asking the caller if she'd checked with the local library for the information. Her response was, "This *is* the library." I knew then that there was a book in this somewhere, so I began compiling a list of authors, illustrators, and storytellers in New Mexico with encouragement and help from Elaine Shannon, then head of programming for the Albuquerque Public Library system. This little "directory" grew into a book listing authors, illustrators, and storytellers from the entire Southwest, and that book grew into a volume of authors, illustrators, and storytellers who wanted to come to the fabled Southwest. So, I have Joe Hayes and Elaine Shannon to thank for bringing this directory into existence.

Presenter Selection

It was determined early in the process of writing this revised and expanded directory that authors, illustrators, and storytellers would be selected for inclusion from many sources and based on many criteria.

Published members of the Society of Children's Book Writers and Illustrators were contacted via e-mail, as were members of the National Association of Storytellers (what used to be NAPPS), the Authors Guild, and the Children's Book Guild. In addition, contacts were solicited from marketing and library personnel at most children's publishing houses. Authors and storytellers helped by spreading the word to their critique groups and professional associations, allowing fellow members an opportunity to submit information. Librarian recommendations and referrals by guilds, such as Women Writing the West and the National Story Guild, were considered. Every person who's listed in this directory responded personally to a request for information.

Numerous storytellers, authors, and illustrators use Web sites as their initial contact method, and we used such sites for that purpose. Please note, however, that we didn't include information in this book about such authors without first obtaining from them explicit permission to do so. We felt that even though publicizing oneself with a Web site constitutes a level of consent—of making information publicly available—it wasn't appropriate to include such information without such authors' permission.

As we searched the Web, we discovered that even though biographical and bibliographical data supposedly can be found at <www.easytofind.com>, detailed booking information for authors, illustrators, and storytellers was *not* easy to find. We discovered, however, that the gigantic publishers have extensive Web sites with listings and links for hundreds of authors and illustrators, and that some of these listings include direct contact information.

Several criteria were used to determine authors' inclusion in this directory. First, we considered whether a presentation, and the books and stories used in it, was appropriate for ages K-12. We also considered whether a presenter was willing to work in schools for a reasonable fee. Another determining factor was performer availability—some Newbery and Caldecott authors, for instance, are booked years in advance or don't visit schools. Additional consideration was given to whether an author, illustrator, or storyteller was experienced with K-12 audiences, teachers, and librarians. Professional affiliation with an organization such as the Authors Guild, the Society of Children's Book Writers and Illustrators, or the National Storytelling Association was a factor, as was accessibility via e-mail and the Web. Every presenter included in this book (thus its title) had to be willing to travel. Most of the performers who are included expressed a resounding eagerness to visit schools far and wide, as long as their expenses and lodging were paid by the sponsoring institution.

All of these sources and criteria, as well as my acquaintance with many of the selected authors through publication of previous directories and 20 years in children's bookselling, combined to make this directory a reality.

Teachers, librarians, and event planners will find *Have Talent Will Travel: A Directory of Author, Illustrators, and Storytellers East of the Mississippi* a unique and an invaluable resource for finding talented, available presenters who visit schools and don't charge a fortune. Aside from spending a hundred hours on the Web, you won't find this much information in any one place.

About the Listings

Entries are listed alphabetically by state, then alphabetically by last name. All of the presenters listed in this directory are experienced with K-12 audiences and have written a brief description of their presentation. If a performer expressed a preference for grade or age level, that's noted in the listing.

We requested the following information from each presenter we contacted: a contact phone/fax (some presenters preferred not to include this information), an e-mail address, a Web site address (if applicable), a description of the school performance, preferred age level (K-12), fee, and three titles with publisher, publishing date, ISBN, and awards (if any).

We also note presenters' needs for equipment such as microphones, slide projectors, etc. Assume the following: If a speaker asks for a slide projector, there's a concomitant need for a screen and a presentation room that can be darkened; if a blackboard or whiteboard is needed, then chalk or markers also are needed. Almost every presenter we list mentioned water as a need, as well as a chair to go with a table. If presenters didn't indicate particular equipment needs for their visits, we omitted that field from their listing, in the interests of brevity.

Titles are hardcover unless otherwise noted.

Presenters' fees (daily stipends) are encoded: each "$" represents $500. Thus, $=$0-500, $$=$500-1,000, $$$=$1,000-1,500, and $$$$=$1,500-2,000. Many presenters asked us to mention that all fees are negotiable.

In addition to the listings, the section, "Tips on Arranging Your Event," summarizes insights gleaned from a variety of sources, including the presenters themselves. The extensive appendix features a list of authors who can be found via the Web, including numerous high-profile presenters. Many of them, however, are only rarely accessible to their adoring audiences because they no longer visit schools or libraries, or are booked years in advance, or can be contacted only through their publisher.

All of this information is designed to help readers make author, illustrator, and storyteller visits to their school or library valuable and memorable events that won't cause personal meltdowns. We welcome your feedback and suggestions for subsequent editions of this unusual volume.

Tips on Arranging Your Event

Author, illustrator, and storyteller visits can be enjoyable and rewarding events if you plan ahead. Outlining every detail of an event that can cost hundreds, even thousands, of dollars is an awesome responsibility. Doing your research, making lists, delegating responsibilities to people whom you know will carry through, making sure that everything is as perfect as if the President were coming to visit, are all points to keep in mind when planning such an event. The payoff? Turning kids on to the power of literature. We highly recommend that you also read *ABC's of an Author/Illustrator Visit* by Sharron L. McElmeel (Linworth, 2001). Here are some of our own guidelines:

- Select your speaker carefully. In collaboration with the school staff, make a list of the most desired or requested authors. Do your research: Gather initial information about your speaker using the Web, publisher information, and traditional research tools, such as *Something About the Author, Booklinks, The Book Report and Library Talk Author Profile Collection*, and publisher catalogs.

- As you scan through this directory seeking presenters whose fees are low or free (indicated by one "$"), don't forget that you're a resourceful person who probably can find funds for an author event. Cost is often the most important consideration when selecting a speaker, but don't be discouraged before seeking additional funding sources. For instance, try to obtain a small grant from a local business to offset the event's expense in return for sponsorship (tasteful and low-key, the way it's done on your local PBS station or NPR affiliate). If you have sufficient lead time, write a grant for the costs involved—such funding may enable you to afford the most expensive speaker. Persuade an airline to donate transportation costs or to let you use pooled frequent-flyer miles from parents in return for acknowledging their sponsorship. If a local bookstore already has an author booked for an autographing, arrange a collaborative event with another school or the local public library, which would lower the overall cost. We highly recommended partnering for these events.

- Read books by the presenter and connect the content to the school's curriculum. This is perhaps the most important aspect to consider (after money) when selecting a presenter, because the whole point of having a real, live speaker come talk to the kids is to create a sense of connection. Brainstorm with staff members for ways to connect the author's books to the classroom beyond language arts and literature. Keep a list of ideas going by posting the list in the teachers' lounge and inviting people to add their ideas to it.

- It's also important to read the presenter's books to ensure that you're choosing a presenter whose message, books, and reputation will be acceptable to your patrons, teachers, parents, and kids. This will help the audience feel connected to the speaker and, through her or him, to a larger world. Naturally, you should try to expand the audience's worldview via your selection of speakers, but you don't want to stir up a tempest in a teapot (or a cauldron) by presenting material that's so controversial it will generate negative publicity and an unwelcome measure of notoriety. Select presenters and subject matter with sensitivity for your audience's worldview.

- Similarly, strive to match presenters' programs with your audience's interests and age level. If, for instance, you choose to present local authors simply because they're local, but their topic of interest turns out to be the principal exports of Namibia, they probably won't be a good fit with your first graders' interests and attention spans.

In addition to these fundamental considerations, the best tips we can give you concern how to deal effectively and courteously with presenters, how to schedule, how to obtain publicity, and how to prepare the site and the audience for author events.

Care and Feeding of a Presenter

Organizing a visit by a speaker is like engineering a visit by royalty. The concerns of protocol and etiquette are soon eclipsed by the logistics of preparation and of making the visit favorably memorable, including site considerations of space, equipment, schedule, and security. Are you going to handle all of this alone? Not likely. You'll need a solid committee of tested volunteers to help you every step of the way. If you've held a book fair, you probably have a bunch of dedicated book lovers you can call on again. Use them well.

What follows are some of the committee tasks you'll want to consider.

First, there are the arrangements for physically getting performers to the events—getting presenters from their doorstep to yours—which need to be handled by someone with a good eye for detail. Who will pay for the airline tickets and when? Will someone pick up presenters or will a cab be waiting? Who will be responsible for sending a current, accurate map to presenters before they depart from home?

Next, do presenters need to be fed? Are school lunches the most appropriate meals for presenters? Are you going to host a special presenter event just for teachers? If so, who will engineer it? Where? When? Are you going to host a dinner in addition to the school-day event? Will it be in a hotel? If so, will there be a fee? Will you have a cash bar for the adults? Are you sure the presenters will have the stamina to attend an evening event?

Where will presenters be housed? Not on your couch, that's for certain—most authors don't want to stay in a private home (unless you run a professional bed and breakfast). Most need the solitude of a hotel room in which to collect their energies. How will presenters get to that housing from the school and thence to the airport? If presenters are driving to your school, will you reimburse them for mileage? If so, how much? Who will give presenters that check?

Speaking of checks, who will make sure that presenters are paid on the day of the performance? Where will the check be cut, when, and by whom? Most presenters expect their expenses (meals, gas, airfare, and hotel) to be paid for by their host. They also expect to be paid their honorarium before they leave: *don't* mail the check later. Similarly, don't expect presenters to submit expense reports to you for later reimbursement. Presenters don't usually take purchase orders for school visits, nor do they have the resources to pay for their expenses and wait 10 weeks for payment.

Finally, what do presenters want from the schools they visit more than anything? To feel wanted and welcomed. At schools that truly support author events, you're likely to see at least some of the following:

- Banners welcoming the visitor by name.
- Cameras on hand and loaded.
- Stacks of the presenter's books, biographies, and other evidence of the difference the authors and their work have made to students, everywhere in the school—even in the bathrooms.
- Bulletin board and hallway displays that celebrate the creations of the visiting artist.
- A videotape of the presenter (if available) that's been seen by all of the classes, the staff, and even the janitor and the principal.
- A sense of celebration and anticipation.
- Evidence of thorough planning and a sense of dignified preparation, not hysterical, last-minute dashing, hither and thither.
- Kids are encouraged to compare titles by same author.
- Kids writing "copycat" stories in the author's style, writing a new ending, or making paintings and pictures that relate to the author's work.
- Kids and teachers reaching for connections with math, science, physical education, music, geography, and history.
- Teachers helping kids compile lists of questions for presenters and research answers to as many as they can before the event.
- Kids engaging in "battle of the books" events about authors to earn the honor of having lunch with them.

Nuts & Bolts

Scheduling

When setting a date for your author event, start with the calendar. Check, then double-check, to make sure you're using this year's calendar. Verify that you're not competing with a teachers' convention, a major sporting event, a release day, or the neighborhood's biggest event of the year. Don't inadvertently schedule an author event on Election Day, if your school hosts voting booths. Call the appropriate government authorities to determine that your event doesn't conflict with the landing of aliens from Mars or any other scheduled or anticipated events. Ensure that *your* event is the biggest thing going on that day.

Once a date is set, schedule and outline the event so that the school day is used to best advantage. Consider when you want to start. If the presenter has to drive three hours before the program begins at 8 a.m., he or she will be in less than prime condition upon arrival. If you must start early or run late, make arrangements for the speaker to stay in a hotel/motel. Speaking is hard work, and few speakers can do more than four presentations in a day and live to tell about it, so set a reasonable schedule. Also, presenters can't go nonstop; they need potty breaks, lunch breaks, and coffee breaks.

Before the program, think about who will introduce the presenter, when and how that introduction will take place, and have a backup plan. When the presenter arrives, give him or her a warm welcome, a chair, a glass, and a pitcher of water.

How long will it take to plan your event? Here's a timetable for an author, illustrator, or storyteller visit.

One year in advance:

- ❏ Select authors based on staff recommendations, Web research, appropriate content for the grade level, and school milieu.
- ❏ Contact individual authors, either through this directory or through publishers or Web sites.
- ❏ Seek funding sources and approval.
- ❏ Set dates and times, making sure to coordinate with the school calendar to avoid conflict with vacation, conferences, testing, and competing community events.
- ❏ Send a letter of agreement or a contract to the selected presenter that stipulates dates, times, number of sessions, and costs (this is not a final schedule).

Three months in advance:

- ❏ Contact the presenter to obtain a photo and the title of the presentation for publicity purposes.
- ❏ Request biographical information and a copy of the author's signature (to make bookmarks or bookplates).
- ❏ Request free posters, bookmarks, galleys, and book covers from the publisher's publicity department.
- ❏ List the equipment that will be needed by the presenter, then reserve the appropriate equipment.
- ❏ Set the schedule for the visit (clear it with staff).

- ❏ Collect resources for teachers: at least two copies of each book for the library and enough copies for classrooms. (Hint: When you catalog all of these copies, put them under a single material type in the online catalog so they show up together.)
- ❏ Prepare a teacher-resource booklet that includes Web page information, lesson plans, the final event schedule, an annotated bibliography, a biography, and any other pertinent material you've found.
- ❏ Order books for the author signing from the publisher or the local jobber, book store, or wholesaler.
- ❏ If a dinner event is part of the schedule, you should be well into the process of finding a location and making pricing, food, bar, and seating arrangements.

One month in advance:

- ❏ Check with the publisher or author to obtain a reproducible brochure that will go home to all families. The brochure should include a photo, the author's signature, a bibliography, and a list of activity ideas for families to use in advance (e.g., pertinent books, stories, and recipes).
- ❏ Put up hallway bulletin boards and banners.

Two weeks in advance:

- ❏ Obtain the check for the presenter's stipend and travel reimbursement.
- ❏ Decorate library bulletin boards, school doors, and even bathrooms.
- ❏ Purchase a small gift for the author.
- ❏ Obtain and double-check supplies and equipment.
- ❏ Assign adult escorts for the author.
- ❏ Take photos of the staff to give to the author.
- ❏ Announce the event on the school marquee.
- ❏ Schedule a staff luncheon with the author (suggest that everybody bring a dessert). If a dinner is planned, all arrangements should be finalized and in writing with the caterer or hotel.

The day before the event:

- ❏ Make sure the presenter has arrived in one piece.
- ❏ Make sure that the sound equipment hasn't been filched.
- ❏ Make sure all teachers have the event schedule in hand.
- ❏ Make sure the books for sale are secure, that you have start cash and a cash box ready, and that prepaid books are ready for signing.
- ❏ Have cameras ready (Polaroids are especially useful) so that photos can be taken of the author with staff, with classes, and even with individuals.
- ❏ Try to get a good night's sleep (dream on).

The day of the event:

❑ Greet the speaker at the door, show her or him the facilities (including bathroom locations), double-check the venue and equipment.

❑ Have the sales tables and sales people ready for the rush.

❑ Follow the schedule.

❑ Enjoy the day! You've earned it!

Booksigning & Selling

The sale of autographed books, tapes, videos, etc. can pay for the presenter's stipend if you plan well. Assuming that you plan to sell such items, who will do the math to figure out how many books you need to sell to pay for the author visit? Who will create an order form to pre-sell copies of authors' books so that enough copies will be paid for, on hand, and available to autograph on the Big Day? Who will do the incoming physical count? Who will get the start cash? Who will handle the actual sales? Who will get the bags? Who will do the final sales tally and ending inventory? Who will deposit the cash? If the speaker gets a cut (or all) of the money, who will write that check? Will that person be available when you need the check to be signed?

Ordering goods to sell is like opening a bookstore for a day. Who will order the books, posters, cards, videos, or tapes and CDs? From where will they be ordered? What's the best discount you can get? What's the company's return policy? Who will physically receive the shipments? Who will physically return the leftovers? If you're collaborating with a local bookstore or book-fair jobber, who will heave those 50-pound boxes of books in and out of the truck? Who will dolly them to the autographing site? Who will make sure the prices are posted and that those prices match what's on the books? Who will deal with the inevitably missing books that seem to have been shipped to another planet?

If books are selling like hotcakes, what if somebody brings a stack of tattered copies from another library to be signed? If the speaker is a storyteller with CDs or tapes instead of books, how are those products autographed? How long will presenters be able to sign? What if there are still books to be signed when the time allotted for autographs is up?

If you don't plan to sell presenters' books, etc. at the event (which would chagrin almost every author, illustrator, and storyteller in this book), alternatives to book sales must be considered. What memento will be available for kids and teachers? Will posters be available for signing? (Most authors really hate signing slips of paper.)

Who will make sure that the sales table is sturdy, so that it doesn't wobble when eager book buyers lean against it, trying to get as close as possible to the author? Who will sit next to the authors and hold books open so that they can easily be signed? Who will make sure that the requested inscriptions are written legibly on slips of paper so names can be properly spelled? Who will make sure there are extra pens on hand? What will you do about kids who can't afford a book and want authors to sign something else, instead? Who will make sure that sturdy bookmarks are already copied for such a contingency? Who will supply 3 x 5-inch, self-stick, plain labels that the author can sign as "bookplates" for parents who show up after the event and say, "Oh, I thought the signing was today"? How about the child who shows up with a check, which his parents FedExed from their hotel in Paris (really, this actually happened!), for a signed book, but the author is long gone?

Publicity

Even more than detailed planning, publicity is perhaps the most important factor in determining whether or not your event will succeed. But publicity is the hardest job to do because there's no sure formula. Who will write and print press releases, then get them to the appropriate person at local newspapers, TV stations, and radio stations? Who will make the follow-up calls to ensure that said media will let the whole world know that your school is sponsoring this once-in-a-lifetime opportunity? Who will dog the TV stations to send a camera crew to shoot film of your student parade of favorite book characters? Who will pay for newspaper ads? Or, who will make sure that freebie announcements actually get into print?

Who will make sure written invitations are sent to local officials and notables? Who will make sure that parent notes are actually received by parents? Who will make sure to invite staff and librarians from other libraries or schools? Who will be in charge of taking tons of photos of the presenters in action and later turning those into scrapbook pages or downloading them onto the school's Web page?

Site Preparation & Equipment

Pay close attention when setting up the presentation site.

Where will the performance take place? How will you group the kids and how large will the groups be? If you have to use the all-purpose room, how will you work around the cafeteria schedule and still feed all of the kids? How will you seat them so that shuffling chair legs won't drown out the performance? Can you cram everyone into the library? How long will it take to seat all those first graders who've never done this before? Do you put the big kids in the back or the front?

Make sure the room is suitable for the purpose and that the sound system works. Most presenters can't be heard across the rumble of 500 kids without some sort of sound amplification. Who will obtain and set up the microphone, mike stand, amplifier, and speakers, then test the equipment ahead of time, in the presentation space, to make sure that everything works, that the extension cord is long enough, and that the electrical socket is supplying juice? Who will run the soundboard, to make sure that the volume isn't causing the loose teeth to drop out of the mouths of the little kids in the front row, while simultaneously causing the big busters in the back to mutiny because they can hear only every other word? Who will videotape the event (if the speaker has granted permission) without upstaging the live audience?

Many presenters require slide projectors. It goes without saying that they also need a screen and a presentation space that can be sufficiently darkened so that the audience can see the projected images. Who will find the screen and make sure it doesn't collapse unpredictably? Who will test the blinds to make sure that the daylight doesn't wash out the images? Who will make sure that extra projector bulbs will be on hand, that they fit the projector, and that somebody knows how to change them? (Equipment knows Murphy's Law: The only time the slide-projector bulb will burn out or blow up is when the guest you've spent so much time, energy, and money getting to this point is "on stage," and nowhere in the building, or even the county, can you find a replacement bulb.) Who will make sure the extension cords are grounded, so the fire department doesn't show up as uninvited entertainment?

Who will be the backup for all of the above when the person who said they'd do these jobs goes into early labor, comes down with the flu, or just doesn't show up?

Audience Preparation

Student preparation, along with presenter accommodations, scheduling, publicity, and site preparation, is another key to a successful event. Engineering interaction between audience members and presenters is seldom mentioned in event-planning material, but should be given some thought. Who will take charge of moving the speaker from one place to the next place on the schedule? We assume teachers are behind the event 1,000%, but who will make sure that adequate numbers of copies of presenters' books get to teachers ahead of time, so that everyone will be familiar with the speakers' works by the time the speakers arrive? Who will make sure that teachers have the support materials they need and the time to share the materials they've gathered? Who will make sure the curriculum connections are made?

Who will prepare the students by rehearsing the actual presentation and signing? It's said that an army moves on its stomach, but that a performer moves on wings of tactfulness. How many of the students have attended a live presentation and know the appropriate etiquette? Do they know that it's not polite to ask the speaker how old he/she is, or how much money he/she makes? What if a kid has to go to the bathroom during the performance? Who will teach the kids how to behave when authors ask for a show of hands or a volunteer? Many audience members assume that presenters would love to read the little story they wrote about their cat Fluffy. Who will act as the trusty sidekick (escort) for the author and head off these eager wannabes? Who will tactfully tell kids (and grown-ups) that authors can't autograph their lunch napkins?

Put It in Writing

Attend carefully to the details, finalize the arrangements with presenters, then put it all in writing—and don't change the plan once it's been agreed to.

Make sure you and the presenter agree on the exact length of each session, the length of the break between sessions, and the ages of audience members. If a presenter is traveling some distance, be exact and clear about who's planning the travel arrangements and whose travel is covered (some presenters travel with spouses or families). Send a map, exact directions, and phone numbers to the presenter well in advance of the visit. Include the phone number of a "real, live person" and a non-daytime number for an event planner, in case of emergency. If the author is to appear in more than one location, spell out whose responsibility it will be to provide transportation to each site. If you've a printed program, send a copy to the presenter. This helps speakers avoid duplicating each other on mixed-bill programs. Give presenters information about the audience well in advance of their program.

Remember: always say "thank you"! You may want to have students send personalized letters. If so, make sure the kids write real thank-you notes, not canned correspondence they copy from the blackboard. Never send an evaluation of a speaker's performance to a speaker, even if you have one. Even if the presentation was a disappointment, never let your guest receive a negative or damaging comment.

After all is said and done, remember that authors and illustrators and storytellers aren't Hollywood entertainers. Their fees are usually reasonable. Their job is to make reading fashionable and fun, to make books a vital and exciting part of kids' lives, and to help bring stories to the forefront of their audience's attention. Take good care of them and they'll reward your efforts many times over.

The Payoff

This seems like a lot of work—and it is. So why bother?

Look at it this way. Our world is filled with information and possibility, which is wonderful, but which also generates feelings of fragmentation and disconnection. Television disgorges endless amounts of garbage and, paradoxically, the richest source of information the planet has ever seen—the World Wide Web—simultaneously increases the isolation of learners. Giving children the opportunity to meet the person who wrote their favorite book, or drew its pictures, or who tells a mind-expanding story can be a major turning point in children's lives. Author events help kids connect to books, reading, ideas, and a lifetime's enjoyment of the written word.

School visits by live artists can enhance student learning and enrich the curriculum. They aren't frivolous events for which kids get to abandon their classroom tasks. Meeting actual authors, illustrators, and storytellers can teach kids all sorts of things they otherwise would never get a chance to absorb, everything from how to shake hands properly and introduce themselves (and others) to how much hard work goes into making a book a reality.

All of these reasons should provide you with plenty of payoff for the hard work involved in arranging author, illustrator, or storyteller visits.

My final advice? Take lots of pictures, sell lots of books, and have lots of good memories.

Alabama

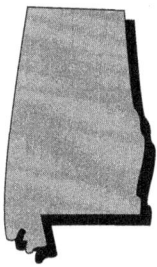

Joan Broerman

1616 Kestwick Drive
Birmingham, AL 35226
<members.home.net/joanbroerman/>

Joan Broerman's interactive presentation engages young authors by helping them become a community of writers who respect and encourage mutual growth. Everybody writes!

- Grade levels: K-12
- $-$$
- *Weekend Getaways in Alabama.* Pelican Publishing, 2000, ISBN 1565546768
- Requirements: Sound system, lavalier microphone

Charles Ghigna

204 West Linwood Drive
Homewood, AL 35209
(205) 870-4261
(205) 870-0250 fax
PaGoose@aol.com
<www.charlesghigna.com>

Charles Ghigna, a.k.a. Father Goose, is a nationally syndicated writer and the author of more than 20 books of poetry for kids. His award-winning books have been featured on *Good Morning America*, nominated for a Pulitzer Prize, and featured at Scholastic bookfairs. He's presented his poetry at the Library of Congress; the John F. Kennedy Center; and hundreds of schools, libraries, and colleges in the U.S. and overseas.

- Grade levels: K-12
- $$$
- *One Hundred Shoes.* Random House, 2002, ISBN 0375821783

  Mice Are Nice. Random House, 1999, ISBN 0679989293
- Requirements: Sound system, table

Jo Kittinger

1612 Colesbury Circle
Hoover, AL 35226
(205) 823-2970
(810) 283-6300 fax
jskittinger@bellsouth.net

Nonfiction Is Fun! Dead Log Alive! Look at Rocks and Minerals, and *Reading is Fun!* are some of Jo Kittinger's presentations, in which she shares her research, discoveries, and delights. Her creative writing workshops stress the use of sensory detail, character development, and plot.

- Grade levels: K-6
- $
- *Going to the Beach.* Children's Press, 2002, ISBN 0516225359

  Birds of North America East. DK Publishing, 2001, ISBN 0789478986, 0789478994 pbk

  A Look at Rocks: From Coal to Kimberlite. Franklin Watts, 1997, ISBN 0531203107, 053115887x pbk, Best Science Books for Children 1998
- Requirements: Overhead projector, table

Claudia Pearson

2461 Mountain Vista
Birmingham, AL 35243
(205) 823-8556
pearsoncrz@earthlink.net

Claudia Pearson is a writer, teacher, and former lawyer who discusses writing and storytelling experiences in her three careers, including the use of "grabber" leads, effective storytelling techniques, and generating visual images through description. As part of her presentation for younger students, she includes opportunities for them to create illustrations for her stories. With older students, she discusses the similarities and differences in lawyers' and writers' careers, as well as how stories get published.

- Grade levels: K-12
- $

Connecticut

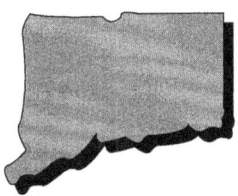

Tony Abbott

49 Chestnut Hill Road
Trumbull, CT 06611
(203) 452-7804 phone/fax
theabbotts@att.net
<www.tonyabbottbooks.com>

Tony Abbott's lively presentations on creative writing use humor and adventure to draw young people into the pleasures of reading and writing. He offers a variety of writing-related topics, including *Tapping Your Imagination, Fundamentals of Storytelling, Living Beyond the Page,* and *Keeping the Story Moving,* as well as a slide show, *A Day in the Life of a Writer.*

- Grade levels: 1-5
- $$
- *Secrets of Droon* series, Scholastic, more than 13 titles
- Requirements: Slide cart, screen, lapel microphone (brings his own projector)

Suzanne I. Barchers

104 North Street, #303
Stamford, CT 06912
(203) 975-8465
(203) 705-1661 fax
sbarchers@aol.com
<www.storycart.com>

Suzanne Barchers, author of 18 books for teachers and librarians and 22 books for children, provides students with insights into the many facets of being an author and editor. She's also the managing editor of *Weekly Reader* and her presentations explore all aspects of the magazine and publishing worlds. She takes students through the publishing process, from getting an idea to writing the book, to finding a publisher, to marketing the product.

- Grade levels: 3-6
- $-$$
- *From Atalanta to Zeus: Readers Theater from Greek Mythology.* Teacher Ideas Press, 2001, ISBN 1563088150

  Leaps, Hops, Pops and Mops. Leapfrog Schoolhouse, 2000, ISBN 1586050176

  Cooking Up U.S. History. Teacher Ideas Press, 1999, ISBN 1563086824

Nora Raleigh Baskin

87 Birch Hill Road
Weston, CT 06883
(203) 226-6079
(203) 226-7061 fax
Norabaskin@aol.com
<www.norabaskin.com>

Nora Baskin offers unusual and honest insight into the dream of becoming a writer when she visits schools by sharing her own sixth grade journals and diaries. Her stories of being the child who never fit in lead to her recounting of nine years of rejections—then finally being published by writing the book that was in her heart. She inspires students to never give up, whatever their dreams might be.

- Grade levels: K-8
- $
- *What Every Girl (Except Me) Knows.* Little Brown, 2001, ISBN 0316070211, Booklist Top Ten Youth Novels, *Publishers Weekly* Cuffie Award Most Promising New Author, Booksense list 2001

Carol L. Birch

32 B Heritage Circle
Southbury, CT 06488
(203) 264-3800
(914) 238-3597 fax
cbirch@westchesterlibraries.org

Carol Birch is a superb storyteller in matters of the heart, and her audiences respond to her infectious enthusiasm, artistry, and clarity. Her repertoire includes unusual adaptations of America's greatest writers—Sandburg, Bradbury, Steinbeck—and vibrant retellings of folktales. She's won the National Storytelling Network Circle of Excellence Award, the Southern Connecticut State University Millennium Award, and an Outstanding Educator Award. She's appeared as a featured storyteller at national festivals, on television, radio, and even in the *New York Times*.

- Grade levels: K-12
- $-$$$ (greatly reduced rates for libraries)
- *The Whole Story Handbook: Using Imagery to Complete the Story Experience.* August House, 2000, ISBN 0874835666, *Storytelling World* Gold Award

  Who Says? Essays on Pivotal Issues in Contemporary Storytelling. Co-editor with Melissa Heckler, August House, 1996, *Storytelling World* Honor Book, The Anne Izard Storytellers' Choice Award

  Careful What You Wish For. Cassette, self-published, no ISBN
- Requirements: Microphone with substantial cord or range of movement

Lisa Rowe Fraustino

75 C Eastbrook Heights
Mansfield Center, CT 16250
(860) 423-5856
Authorash@aol.com
<hometown.aol.com/authorash>

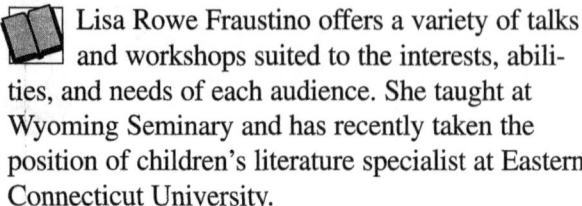

Lisa Rowe Fraustino offers a variety of talks and workshops suited to the interests, abilities, and needs of each audience. She taught at Wyoming Seminary and has recently taken the position of children's literature specialist at Eastern Connecticut University.

- Grade levels: K-12
- $$
- *Soul Searching: Thirteen Stories about Faith and Belief.* Simon & Schuster, 2002, forthcoming

  The Hickory Chair. Illustrated by Benny Andrews, Scholastic, 2001, ISBN 0590522485, Bulletin for the Center for Children's Books Blue Ribbon, Oppenheimer Gold Award

  Dirty Laundry: Stories about Family Secrets. Viking, 1998, ISBN 0670879118, American Library Association Quick Pick for Reluctant Readers, New York Public Library Best Book for the Teen Age
- Requirements: Slide projector, overhead projector

Drew Gibson

145 East Avenue
Norwalk, CT 06851
(203) 838-5541
(888) 240-8381
drewgibson@snet.net
<mythology.netfirms.com>

Drew Gibson performs classics—epic mythology from Greece and India; 19th-century American history; and western literature such as *Uncle Tom's Cabin*, Dickens' *Christmas Carol*, and stories from the Civil War in Kansas.

- Grade levels: 5-12
- $$
- *Stories from Greek Mythology.* Cassette, self-published, no ISBN

John Himmelman

17 Hunters Ridge Road
Killingworth, CT 06419
(860) 663-3225 phone/fax
jhimmel@mindspring.com
<www.johnhimmelman.com>

 Writer and illustrator John Himmelman has come up with three ways to make the blank piece of paper less daunting, and he shares his secrets with students. He also offers a slide show about the animals he used to create his stories, in order to inspire students as observers. A session titled *The Mailbox Is My Friend* examines what it's like to make a living as an author and illustrator and explains how to deal with the three big enemies: temptation, procrastination, and deadlines.

- Grade levels: 1-12
- $$

- *Pipaluk and the Whales*. National Geographic, 2002, ISBN 0792282175

 A Pill Bug's Life. Childrens Press, 1999, ISBN 051621165, National Science Teachers Association Outstanding Science Trade Book

 Wanted: Perfect Parents. Troll, 1993, ISBN 0816730296

Patricia Hubbell

90 Norton Road
Easton, CT 06612
(203) 268-8128
pathubbell@kidspoet.com
<www.kidspoet.com> or <www.pathubbell.com>

Pat Hubbell tells kids how she began writing poetry by sitting up in a tree and watching a fox play in a meadow. She reads her poems, tells how they came about, and discusses poetic strategies. Students learn how to find dozens of poetry subjects in the classroom, how to turn a story into a poem, and why poets like to add and subtract. Pat is the author of nine poetry books, and her work appears in several hundred anthologies.

- Grade levels: 2-4
- $

- *Rabbit Moon*. Marshall Cavendish, 2002, ISBN 076145103x

Black Earth Gold Sun. Marshall Cavendish, 2001, ISBN 0761450904

Earthmates. Marshall Cavendish, 2000, ISBN 0761450629

Kathleen V. Kudlinski

95 Alden Drive
Guilford, CT 06437
(203) 457-9187
kathkud@aol.com
<www.kathleen-v-kudlinski.com>

Kathleen Kudlinski's lively programs are sprinkled with amusing anecdotes and practical tips gleaned from writing 23 science, biography, and historical fiction books for children, as well as an award-winning newspaper column on nature. Her storycrafting session shows how to create original characters, tension-filled plots, and satisfying conclusions; other sessions teach students about bringing history and nature to life on paper.

- Grade levels: K-6
- $$

- *Boy, Were We Wrong About Dinosaurs!* Dutton, 2002, ISBN 0525469788

 Harriet Tubman: Freedom's Trailblazer. Simon & Schuster, 2002, ISBN 0689848668

 Earthquake! A Story of Old San Francisco. Viking, 2000, ISBN 01400353904

Louise Ladd

27 Bloomfield Drive
Fairfield, CT 06432
(203) 336-9323
louiseld@optonline.net

Louise Ladd writes books packed with action and humor. Her presentations reveal a writing world where surprises and amusing adventures keep the characters (and readers) on their toes. This former actress and part-time librarian says she became a writer so she could go to work in her bathrobe.

- Grade levels: 3-7
- $$

Double Diamond Dude Ranch series (8 titles), Tor, 2002 (titles include *Call Me Just Plain Chris, The Wrangler's Secret, Prize-winning Horse—Maybe, The Perfect Horse, Rodeo, Me My Mare and the Movie, Home for Christmas, Belle's Foal*), various ISBNs

Betsy and Giulio Maestro

74 Mile Creek Road
Old Lyme, CT 06371
(860) 434-9773
(860) 434-1620 fax
BCMAES@aol.com or maestrobooks@aol.com
<www.maestrobooks.com>
<www.authorsillustrators.com>

The Maestro's lively motivational programs take students through the steps of creating nonfiction, from research to finished book. They use visuals to illustrate the importance of research, and the time and hard work required to edit words and art. The Maestros inspire kids to think of themselves as researchers, writers, and artists, and they present editing as a positive cooperative process leading to better writing.

- Grade levels: K-12
- $$$
- *Struggle for a Continent: The French and Indian Wars, 1689-1763*. HarperCollins, 2000, ISBN 0688134513

  The Story of Clocks and Calendars. Lothrop Lee & Shepard, 1999, ISBN 0688145493

  The New Americans: Colonial Times, 1620-1689. Lothrop Lee & Shepard, 1998, ISBN 0688143391
- Requirements: Two tables, microphone

Bobbi Miller

175 Bebbington Road
Ashford, CT 06278
(860) 487-7624
bobbi.miller6@att.net

 Bobbi Miller offers workshops on a wide variety of topics, including using graphic novels to engage young adults, using folklore in the classroom, and storytelling as a means of teaching by using an organic, sense-making approach. She also can discuss folklore and astronomy, family history, mystery, and stories to help students appreciate nature.

- Grade levels: K-12
- $$
- *Miss Sally Ann and the Panther.* Holiday House, forthcoming

  Jasper and the Talking Turtle. Holiday House, forthcoming

  Davy Gets Hitched. Holiday House, forthcoming

Pegi Dietz Shea

27 Fox Hill Drive
Rockville, CT 06066
(860) 872-3513 phone/fax
Deitzshea@aol.com

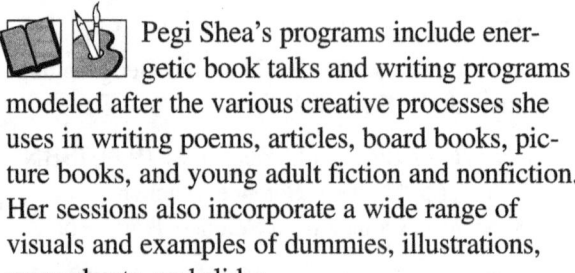 Pegi Shea's programs include energetic book talks and writing programs modeled after the various creative processes she uses in writing poems, articles, board books, picture books, and young adult fiction and nonfiction. Her sessions also incorporate a wide range of visuals and examples of dummies, illustrations, press sheets, and slides.

- Grade levels: K-8
- $$
- *The Shell of the Snail.* Clarion, forthcoming

  Carpet Boy. Tilbury House, forthcoming

  The Whispering Cloth: A Refugee's Story. Boyds Mills Press, 1995, ISBN 1563971348, International Reading Association Teacher's Choice, International Reading Association Notable Book for a Global Society, National Council of Social Studies and Children's Book Council Notable, National Council of Teachers of English Notable
- Requirements: Carousel slide projector, overhead projector, microphone, sometimes TV/VCR

Sanna Stanley

1118 Main Street, #1
Branford, CT 06405
(203) 483-6976
smsanna@aol.com
<www.Two-Ems.com/Sanna.htm>

 Sanna Stanley's upbringing in rural Africa gave her an unusual perspective on multicultural living, a perspective that she shares in her books and talks. *Growing Up in the Congo*, her slide presentation of personal anecdotes about living in the African bush, challenges students to consider the differences and similarities between their culture and another, with questions such as, "Would you eat a snake steak for dinner?" "Would you sweep a dirt floor clean?" Sanna also offers a workshop on the process of writing and illustrating.

- Grade levels: K-6

- $$

- *Monkey for Sale.* Farrar, Straus & Giroux, 2002, ISBN 0374350175

  Monkey Sunday: A Story from a Congolese Village. Farrar, Straus & Giroux, 1998, ISBN 0374350183

Joan C. Verniero

25 Bart Road
Monroe, CT 06468
Jvstory@aol.com
<www.Jvstory.com>

Mythology anyone? Joan Verniero helps kids find a new path into multicultural literature by experiencing the oldest tales from various cultures and seeking similar themes, characters, and adventures in them. Her *So You Want to Know About Children's . . .* books helps listeners learn about the factors of quality, literary elements, and craftsmanship in writing. *You Can Call Me Willy*, a story for children about AIDS, focuses on compassion, friendship, and how to deal with fear, caution, toilet seats, and baseball.

- Grade levels: K-12

- $$

- *101 Read-Aloud Celtic Myths and Legends.* Black Dog and Leventhal, 2000, ISBN 1579120989

  101 Asian Read-Aloud Myths and Legends. Black Dog and Leventhal, 2000, ISBN 1579120989

  You Can Call Me Willy. Magination Press, 1995, ISBN 0945354606

Delaware

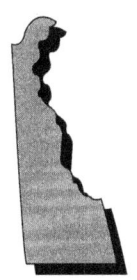

Mary Kennedy

603 Kilburn Road
Wilmington, DE 19803
localcat@msn.com

Mary Kennedy is the author of 28 books for young adult and middle grade readers. Her doctorate in psychology allows her to bring an unusual viewpoint to creativity, brainstorming, and writing. Every child who participates in her interactive session, which includes writing, games, and puzzles, gets a "star for a day" certificate at the end.

- Grade levels: 4-12
- $
- *Mystery in Washington, D.C.* Albert Whitman, 1994, ISBN 0807554049x

  Mystery of the Hidden Beach. Albert Whitman, 1991, ISBN 0807554049

  Mystery of the Lost Village. Albert Whitman, 1989, ISBN 0807554014

Florida

Holly Bea

2904 West Hawthorne Road
Tampa, FL 33611
(813) 805-7445
(813) 835-6511 fax
hbweaver@ix.netcom.com

Holly Bea isn't just an author, advertising copywriter, and creative director—she's a lively speaker who inspires kids to pursue careers in writing. What can a writer do? Write Web site content, create TV commercials, name products, write ads, pen TV shows, and write books—which are just some of the possibilities she encourages youngsters to consider.

- Grade levels: K-8
- $
- *Bless Your Heart.* H. J. Kramer/Starseed Press, 2001, ISBN 0915811944, Helen Keating Ott Award for outstanding contribution to children's literature promoting high ethical and moral values to children

  Good Night, God. H. J. Kramer/Starseed Press, 2000, ISBN 0915811847

  Where Does God Live? H. J. Kramer/Starseed Press, 1997, ISBN 0915811731
- Requirements: Overhead projector

Marianne Berkes

4949 SE Inkwood Way
Hobe Sound, FL 33455
(561) 781-2190 phone/fax
Mberkesbooks@aol.com
<www.geocities.com/mberkesbooks>

Marianne Berkes, a children's librarian and a teacher, is also a musician and a storyteller who enjoys discussing why she wrote *Marsh Music,* while teaching students how to imitate frog sounds and join in the "frog orchestra." Her love of nature, music, and the theater shine through each performance.

- Grade levels: K-4
- $
- *Marsh Morning.* Illustrated by Robert Noreika, Millbrook, 2003, ISBN 0761319360

  Seashells by the Seashore. Illustrated by Robert Noreika, Dawn Publications, 2002, ISBN 1584690356, 1584690348 pbk

  Marsh Music. Illustrated by Robert Noreika, Millbrook, 2000, ISBN 076131850x
- Requirements: VCR with large-screen TV, CD player (for frog sounds)

Myra A. Davis and Phyllis NeSmith

1630 Oleander Place
Bartow, FL 33830-7227
(863) 533-7469
myrastory@aol.com
<www.storyteller.net>

Working together as the Peace River Tale Spinners, Myra Davis and Phyllis NeSmith share the joy of story with all ages to encourage understanding and acceptance of other cultures.

- Grade levels: K-12
- $$
- Requirements: Two microphones, stool

Ken Derby

7771 Pine Trace
Sarasota, FL 34243
(407) 491-7121
kd@kenderby.com
<www.kenderby.com>

International address:
ASIB PO Box 53
Budapest, Hungary 1525

Ken Derby teaches in Budapest, but when he comes home to the States he loves to visit stateside schools, where he talks about writing and books.

- Grade levels: 3-12
- $
- *The Ghost Memoirs of Robert Falcon Scott.* Royal Fireworks, 1999, ISBN 0880925523

Bill Farnsworth

1396 Roosevelt Drive
Venice, FL 34293
(941) 493-1360
bookillustrator@aol.com
<www.billfarnsworth.com>

Bill Farnsworth's presentation *Without Words* gives audiences a glimpse into how he creates his realistic oils on canvas for the books he's illustrated by telling the story without words. Bill's a graduate of the Ringling School of Art and Design and a member of the Society of Illustrators. He "takes" students to his studio through a slide show and takes them through a step-by-step process to create a children's book.

- Grade levels: 2-8
- $$
- *A Humble Life: Plain Poems.* By Linda Oatman, Eerdmans, 2002, ISBN 0802852076

The Great Stone Face. Eerdmans, 2002, ISBN 0802851940

Abbie Against the Storm. Beyond Words, 2002, ISBN 1582700079, Texas Blue Bonnet Award, Young Hoosiers Award nominee

- Requirements: Slide projector, easels

Kathy Feeney

15318 Sherwood Forest Drive
Tampa, FL 33647
(813) 975-9194
Kfeeney777@aol.com

Kathy Feeney shares her passion for reading and writing with students while she teaches them how an idea becomes a book, why writers must write and then rewrite, and how reading and writing can take you where you want to go. Kathy was a newspaper reporter for many years and is the author of more than 25 nonfiction children's books, as well as a winner of the William Randolph Hearst Award for Feature Writing (1980).

- Grade levels: K-12
- $$
- *Alabama.* Children's Press, 2002, ISBN 051223143
- *Manatees.* Creative Publishing, 2001, ISBN 1559717785
- *Television.* Enslow, 2001, ISBN 0766016447

Marcia S. Freeman

4668 Sweetmeadow Circle
Sarasota, FL 34238
(941) 924-6828
mikeandmarcy@compuserve.com
<www.maupinhouse.com>

Marcia Freeman holds students' attention with tales of her rural childhood and attending a one-room school, while she shares details of how these experiences find their way into her books. She surprises students by using science tidbits sprinkled with secrets of writing in her presentation *The Story Behind the Books,* which shows how much fun writing can be. She also shares with students the secret of *How to Be a Good Writer in Two Easy Lessons.*

- Grade levels: K-5
- $
- *The Gift.* Maupin House, 2002, ISBN 0929895517

  Catfish and Spaghetti. Maupin House, 1998, ISBN 0929895215

  Wetlands. Newbridge, 1998, ISBN 1567843816
- Requirements: Overhead projector, table

Judy Gail

13411 SW 112th Lane
Miami, FL 33186
(305) 387-3683
(305) 383-3959 fax
judygailstories@cs.com
<www.judygailstoryteller.com>

Judy Gail, an internationally acclaimed storyteller, offers programs such as *Around the World in Story and Song, Florida Lore, Tales with Ancient Answers to Scientific Questions,* and more. She's known as the "Trouble-making Troubador" because she presents historical programs about people who dared to make a difference, such as *Three Pioneer Women of Florida,* as part of a Florida State Touring Program grant, and *Watchie Esta Hutrie: The Life and Times of Ivy Stranahan.*

- Grade levels: K-12
- $$-$$$$
- *Day of the Moon Shadow: Tales with Ancient Answers to Scientific Questions.* Poppykettle Enterprises, 1995, ISBN 1563083485

  Work and Labor: A History in Story and Song from the Stone Age to the Information Age. Poppykettle Enterprises, 1994, ISBN 1563084090
- Requirements: Sound system with two inputs, table for props

Kathlyn Gay

11633 Bayonet Lane
New Port Richey, FL 34654
(727) 856-3024
kgay@microd.com
<ourworld.compuserve.com/homepages/Kathy>

Kathlyn Gay has been writing professionally for more than 40 years and has more than 100 books published. Nonetheless, her life continues to be enriched by writing nonfiction work focusing on social and environmental issues, culture, history, communication, and even sports. She discusses the process of writing nonfiction, beginning with research and moving through creating a proposal, writing, and publication. She shares hands-on materials, including manuscripts, edited copy, galley sheets, and book jackets, in her talks with students.

- Grade levels: 6-8
- $
- *Bodymarks: Tattooing, Piercing and Branding.* Millbrook, 2003, ISBN 0761317422

  Silent Death: The Threat of Biological and Chemical Terrorism. Millbrook, 2001, ISBN 0761314660

  Leaving Cuba: From Pedro Pan to Elian. Millbrook, 2000, ISBN 0761314660

Lucinda Hathaway

602 Norton Street
Longboat Key, FL 34228
(941) 383-0216
(941) 383-8931 fax
lucindahathaway@comcast.net

When Lucinda Hathaway and her daughter visited a museum in Ocean City, N.J., they found the story of the *Sindia,* a four-masted bark that sank in 1901, just waiting for someone to write it. Lucinda shows slides of the original wreck and weaves the tale of how facts became a full-blown book that describes the saddest and most exciting thing to happen in that little beach town at the time. Lucinda also is an avid naturalist and loves to share tales about Florida wildlife with students.

- Grade levels: 4-6
- $
- *Takashi's Voyage: The Wreck of the Sindia.* Down the Shore Publishing, 1995, ISBN 0945582242

  Float Plan. Study guide to accompany *Takashi's Voyage* (teaches knot tying, sea shanties, Morse code, signal flags, and more), Down the Shore Publishing, 2000, ISBN 0945585528

- Requirements: Carousel slide projector

Gerald Hausman

12699 Cristi Way
Bokeelia, FL 33922
(941) 283-2561
(941) 283-9305 fax
ghausman@compuserve.com
<www.geraldhausman.com>

 Gerald Hausman, a studio recording-arts and sound-effects specialist, enchants students by giving voice to creatures of all kinds. With his daughter, Mariah Fox, he offers a workshop on publishing, illustrating, and writing. He's told ghost stories on the History Channel and has spoken about collecting Native American folktales in the U.S. on National Public Radio. Gerald's won a variety of prestigious awards and accolades for many of his titles.

- Grade levels: K-8
- $$
- *Tom Cringle: The Pirate and the Patriot.* Simon & Schuster, 2001, ISBN 068982811x

  The Jacob Ladder. With Uton Hinds, Orchard Books, 2001, ISBN 0531303314

  The Coyote Bead. Hampton Roads Publishers, 1999, ISBN 1571741453
- Requirements: Sound system, slide projector

Alan N. Kay

5471 Stallion Lake
Palm Harbor, FL 34685
(727) 784-1227
akay@tampabay.rr.com
<www.youngheroesofhistory.com>

The Civil War, Why History? and *Making History Fun* are topics open for discussion with award-winning history teacher Alan Kay, who entertains all ages with his passion for history and his desire to make it fun for students.

- Grade levels: 3-10

- $
- *On the Trail of John Brown's Body.* White Mane Kids, 2002, ISBN 1572492392

  Off to Fight, White Mane Kids, 2002, ISBN 157292406

  Send 'Em South. White Mane Kids, 2001, ISBN 1572492082

Elaine Landau

PO Box 830398
Miami, FL 33283-0398
(305) 596-3757
info@elainelandau.com
<www.elainelandau.com>

In addition to sessions on being an author, Elaine Landau offers a program called *The Titanic Saga,* in which she discusses maritime disasters and tells stories about the Unsinkable Molly Brown. Elaine also offers a presentation on *Ancient Egypt and the Curse of Tutankamen.* She's received numerous National Council for Social Studies and Children's Book Council awards in the fields of science and social studies.

- Grade levels: 3-12
- $$
- *Smokejumpers.* Millbrook Press, 2002, ISBN 0761323244

  Heroine of the Titanic: The Real Unsinkable Molly Brown. Clarion, 2001, ISBN 0395939127, *School Library Journal* starred review

  John F. Kennedy Jr. Millbrook Press, 2000, ISBN 0761318577

Patricia Cronin Marcello

5410 Stoneybrook Lane
Bradenton, FL 34203
(941) 739-8826 phone/fax
patm@patmarcello.com
<www.patmarcello.com>

Pat Marcello wants young people to fall in love with words. She enjoys using her professional background as an instructor for the Institute of Children's Literature to teach kids about the writing life, including giving them practical advice on having their writing published. She offers exercises to encourage participation, leads kids to Web sites where they can learn about writers and writing, and introduces them to a day in the life of a writer.

- Grade levels: 4-8
- $$
- *The Dalai Lama.* Greenwood Press, 2003, ISBN 313322074

  The Navajo. Lucent Books, 2000, ISBN 150066199

  Diana: The Life of a Princess. Andrews McMeel, 1998, ISBN 0836255372
- Requirements: Internet-ready computer

Dominic Martia, Ph.D.

5318 Huntingwood Court
Sarasota, FL 34235
(941) 378-4139
dfmar@webtv.net

Dominic Martia's humorous verse for adults and children is the subject of his talks *How to Play Poetry* and *Rhyming Round Up*, which feature verse narratives and interactive discussions. His work has been published in a variety of magazines and other publications.

- Grade levels: K-12
- $

Gail Radley

875 East Church Street
DeLand, FL 32724
(386) 736-3934
gradley@stetson.edu
<www.stetson.edu/~gradley/>

In her school presentations, Gail Radley discusses endangered animals and ways that students can help save these creatures, including creating poems to communicate their concerns. Gail also shares the journey of one of her works, *Golden Days*, from book to movie.

- Grade levels: K-12
- $
- *Vanishing from Forests and Jungles.* Carolrhoda, 2001, ISBN 0822519372, 1575055678 pbk

  Vanishing from Grasslands and Deserts. Carolrhoda, 2001, ISBN 157505406x, 1575055686 pbk

  Vanishing from the Skies. Carolrhoda, 2001, ISBN 1575054078, 157505566x pbk
- Requirements: PowerPoint computer setup, projector, screen

Gloria Rothstein

6280 Via Palladium
Boca Raton, FL 33433
gloroth@aol.com

Gloria Rothstein writes picture books and books *about* picture books. Her presentations include the *Magic of Writing Picture Books*, *Reading-Writing-and-Reviewing Picture Books*, and *Turning Readers into Writers*.

- Grade levels: K-6
- $
- *Sheep Asleep.* HarperCollins, 2002, ISBN 0060291052

  Real-Life Writing Activities Based on Favorite Picture Books. Scholastic, 2002, ISBN 0439256164

  Read Across America: Exploring 7 Regions Through Popular Children's Literature. Scholastic, 1995, ISBN 0590603418

Maity Schrecengost (S. Maitland)

807 136 Street East
Bradenton, FL 34212
(941) 746-1940
tomandmaity@cs.com

Maity Schrecengost loves research and history. She also loves sharing her writing techniques with adults and students in workshops such as *Let Them Write!*, *Writing Whizardry,* and *Using the Historical Novel in the Classroom.*

- Grade levels: 3-8
- $$
- *Writing Whizardry.* Maupin House, 2001, ISBN 0929895452

  Panther Girl. Maupin House, 1999, ISBN 0929895290, Patrick D. Smith Prize for Florida Literature

- Requirements: Overhead projector, microphone

Brenda Seabrooke

6095 Manasota Key Road
Englewood, FL 34223
seabrooke@ewol.com
<www.childrensbookguild.org>

Brenda Seabrooke uses slides to explain where she finds ideas for her books and discusses the making of a book, including changing plans and conducting research projects, such as burying a Civil War bullet in the front yard. She shows students artifacts, such as a baby-blue dragon (from her book on the care and feeding of dragons), and sometimes shares stories about vampires, ghosts, and history.

- Grade levels: K-12
- $
- *The Haunting at Stratton Falls.* Dutton, 2000, ISBN 0525463895

  The Vampire in My Bathtub. Holiday House, 1999, ISBN 0823415058

  The Haunting of Holroyd Hill. Puffin, 1997, ISBN 0140385401
- Requirements: Carousel slide projector

Wayne and Jane Sims

35 Fullerwood Drive
St. Augustine, FL 32084
(904) 824-8965
(904) 810-2389 fax
storybuff@aol.com
<www.schoolshows.com>

Since 1994, the Sims have shared their eclectic and unusual brand of tandem humor and storytelling with audiences via programs such as *Tributes, Tales and Turnip Greens*; folktales and legends; and stories from the printed page. They also offer storytelling workshops for those who are interested in the gifts of story.

- Grade levels: K-12
- $

Linda Spitzer

5101 SW 65th Avenue
Miami, FL 33155
(305) 665-8429 phone/fax
storybag@aol.com
<www.miamistorytellersguild.com/Linda_spitzer.htm>

Linda Spitzer has captivated her audiences with energetic performances and a vast repertoire of irresistible tales for 15 years in storytelling festivals of all kinds. She also appears weekly as the Biltmore Hotel's "storylady." She's best known for her participatory style of storytelling, Jewish tales of wit and wisdom, and African folktales.

- Grade levels: K-12
- $-$$
- *Sandspun: Florida Folktales by Florida Storytellers.* Pineapple Press, 2001, ISBN 1561642436
- Requirements: Sound system, table

Frank and Mary Lee Sweet

30 Medford Drive
Palm Coast, FL 32137-2504
(386) 446-4909
mlsweet@backintyme.com
sweetml@hotmail.com
<www.backintyme.com>

Backintyme (the Sweets' performance name) illuminates history and folklore through the use of storytelling and music. As Backintyme weaves banjo and folk percussion with stories of the past, their audiences travel back to a different, simpler time. The Sweets' workshops also can include instruction on how to research and develop stories from history, and how to adapt stories for little listeners.

- Grade levels: K-12
- $

Linda Trice

PO Box 17933
Sarasota, FL 34276
TriceDrew@hotmail.com

Dr. Charles Drew, one of the world's most honored scientists, a pioneer of blood plasma, and father of the modern blood bank, devoted his life to puncturing racial myths. In her book and talk, Linda Trice helps students enter Drew's dramatic battles against racism, his triumphs as a student athlete, and his struggle to become a doctor, helping readers and listeners to "dream high."

- Grade levels: 3-12

- $

- *Charles Drew: Pioneer of Blood Plasma.* Bank Street, 2000, ISBN 0071353178

Sylvia Whitman

515 Christor Place
Orlando, FL 32803
(407) 648-5429 phone/fax
sylviawhitman@juno.com

Sylvia Whitman's books lead children into history. Her talks feature discussion about her many articles in *Cobblestone* magazine and her book experiences, and share with students how all writers move from invention through revision to final editing.

- Grade levels: 1-12

- $

- *Children of the World War II Home Front.* Carolrhoda, 2001, ISBN 1575054841

  What's Cooking? The History of American Food. Lerner, 2001, ISBN 0822517329

  Immigrant Children. Carolrhoda, 2000, ISBN 1575053950, Bank Street College Best Children's Books of the Year 2001

- Requirements: PowerPoint setup and/or slide projector

Georgia

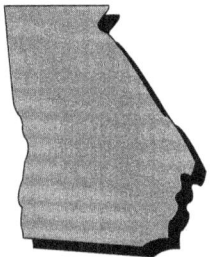

Bess T. Chappas

459 Mall Boulevard, #25
Savannah, GA 31406
(912) 354-7688
savteller@aol.com
<www.geocities.com/savtell>

Bess Chappas came to the U.S. from Athens, Greece, at the age of seven. She loves telling Savannah ghost stories and lore, as well as tales she's collected while traveling to Spain, Italy, France, Great Britain, Egypt, and Russia. She's also developed a workshop for seniors on *Telling Your Own Story*.

- Grade levels: K-12
- $

Patricia Cruzan

115 Clear Creek Court
Fayetteville, GA 30215-4642
(770) 461-9460
patcruzan@aol.com

Using visual aids and the spoken word when describing the writing process empowers readers and writers, according to Pat Cruzan. She shows how the use of organizational structures and "jot lists" provide writers with a framework that helps them learn to develop exciting short stories, articles, and books. Her presentations also can include information on how authors create books, get ideas, and use description.

- Grade levels: K-4
- $-$$

- *Tall Tales of the United States.* Clear Creek, 1996, ISBN 096535430206 lib, 0965354318 pbk

  Sketches of Life. Clear Creek, 1996, ISBN 096535430x

- Requirements: Clip-on microphone, overhead projector, whiteboard or chalkboard, easel, tape player, slide projector

Gail Lerner Karwoski

1040 Sweetgum Way
Watkinsville, GA 30677
(706) 769-8163
(706) 769-9589 fax
gailkarwoski@hotmail.com

 By combining humor, storytelling, fascinating facts, and interactive banter, Gail Karwoski invites students to view history as a collection of great stories about people living through momentous events. Her sessions encourage students to think like writers, to research, to read for inspiration, and to practice writing to increase their communication skills.

- Grade levels: 1-8
- $
- *Surviving Jamestown: The Adventures of Young Sam Collier.* Peachtree, 2001, ISBN 1561452394, 1561452459 pbk

  Seaman, the Dog Who Explored the West with Lewis and Clark. Peachtree, 1999, ISBN 1561451908 pbk, Tennessee Book Award finalist, Georgia Children's Book Award finalist, American Booksellers Association Pick of the Lists

The Tree That Owns Itself and Other Adventure Tales from Georgia's Past. With Loretta Johnson Hammer, Peachtree, 1996, ISBN 1561451207 pbk, Georgia Author of the Year Award for Children's and Young Adult Literature, *Storytelling World* Award

- Requirements: Overhead projector, microphone

Chuck Larkin

175 11th Street NE
Atlanta, GA 30309
(800) 952-7552, code 99
(404) 873-0957 fax (call 800-number first)
mythteller@aol.com
<www.tiac.net/users/papajoe/chuck00.htm>

Chuck Larkin is a bluegrass storyteller, a humorist, a folk singer, and an entertainer who collects and tells traditional stories, folk songs and folklore from 19th century Appalachia, the Piney Woods, and the rural Delta area of the southeastern U.S. He plays a tenor banjo, an old baritone ukelele, a jaw harp, a harmonica, bones, spoons, pan pipes, a didjeridoo, pencils, a nose flute, a sweet-potato flute, and a handsaw played with a fiddle bow. He's told tales that are "nothing but the truth" at hundreds of events during the past three decades.

- Grade levels: K-12
- $
- *Front Porch Storytelling.* Cassettes (three volumes), self-published, no ISBNs

Pamela Bauer Mueller

112 Dunbarton Drive
St. Simons Island, GA 31522
(912) 638-2676 phone/fax
pam@kiskalore.com
<www.kiskalore.com>

Pamela Mueller and her cat, Kiska, wrote true-life adventures of their travels in Mexico, British Columbia, and coastal Georgia, tales that they eagerly share with students. Both Pamela and Kiska are bilingual.

- Grade levels: 1-7
- $

- *Eight Paws to Georgia.* Pinata Publishing, 2001, ISBN 096850972

Rain City Cats. Pinata Publishing, 2000, ISBN 096509711

The Bumpedy Road. Pinata Publishing, 1999, ISBN 096850970-3

Laurie Myers

Augusta, GA
<members.home.net/lauriemyers>

In her school appearances, Laurie Myers shares manuscript samples, artist's drawings, and galley proofs and talks about getting ideas for writing, then developing them into plots. She also discusses the roles of the editor, the illustrator, and the publishing house in the writing process.

- Grade levels: 2-5
- $$
- *Lewis and Clark and Me: A Dog's Tale.* Henry Holt, 2002, ISBN 0805063684

My Dog My Hero. Co-authored by Betsy Byars and Betsy Duffey, Henry Holt, 2000, ISBN 0805063277

Earthquake in the Third Grade. Clarion, 1993, ISBN 0395653606, International Reading Association Children's Choice

Sherry Norfolk

888 Vera Street
Atlanta, GA 30316
(404) 627-7012
(404) 627-8385 fax
shnorfolk@aol.com

Sherry Norfolk is a dynamic storyteller who brings folktales from around the world to life for audiences. Her book-related programs motivate kids to read (as you would expect, given that she spent many years as a children's librarian).

- Grade levels: K-12
- $
- *The Moral of the Story: Folktales for Character Development.* August House, 1999, ISBN 0874835429, 087483550 pbk

Linda Lee Ratto

105 Wheaton Way
Tyrone, GA 30290
(770) 486-0758
(770) 486-6687 fax
RATTO@mindspring.com

Linda Lee Ratto's workshops encourage role-play to help all ages learn how to work with people who live with disabilities. She's a former principal and CEO whose daughter, a congenital amputee, and son, who was blinded in one eye, have inspired her to write children's books and biographies about healthcare professionals.

- Grade levels: K-12
- $
- *Coping with a Physically Challenged Brother or Sister.* Family Counseling Books, 1992, ISBN 0823914925, New York Public Library Best Books for the Teen Age

  Coping with Being Physically Challenged. Family Counseling Books, 1991, ISBN 0823913449

Jo Sanders

4417 Orchard Trace
Roswell, GA 30076
(770) 619-2939
(770) 619-2919 fax
JoStory@aol.com
<www.jostory.com>

Jo Sanders has traveled the world sharing stories with people of other lands in animated and lively performances that are full of humor and suspense. Her presentations include tales of travel, as well as folktales and fairy tales from all over the world.

- Grade levels: K-7
- $
- Requirements: Sound system

Danny Schnitzlein

2658 Spear Point Court
Marietta, GA 30062-2577
(770) 509-3418
dschnitz@mindspring.com

 Students' imaginations soar during Danny Schnitzlein's *Chasing After Monsters* workshop, in which kids discover the steps to writing a story, explore the literature of monsters, learn about careers in writing and art, and get a behind-the-scenes peek into the creation of a picture book. Students also invent characters and draw monsters. In Danny's writing workshops, students learn about the elements that make a successful story, take their "write" brain for a jog, then learn how to edit what they've written. Danny's written for educational television and teaches acrylic painting to all ages.

- Grade levels: K-12
- $
- *The Monster Who Ate My Peas.* Peachtree, 2001, ISBN 1561452165

Diane Z. Shore

4171 Summit Drive
Marietta, GA 30068
(770) 971-1609
DZshore@bellsouth.net
<www.dianezshore.com>

Diane Shore's poetry party begins with her award-winning poem "Get Out of Bed," followed by the recitation and enactment of poetry by Shel Silverstein, Jack Prelutsky, Dr. Seuss, Roald Dahl, and other favorites. Students learn about end rhyme, internal rhyme, meter, rhythm, metaphors, similes, alliteration, assonance, personification, onomatopoeia, hyperbole, and other elements of poems in this energetic performance.

- Grade levels: K-5
- $
- *This Is the Feast.* HarperCollins, forthcoming

  School Bus Bop. Bloomsbury, forthcoming
- Requirements: Easel

Susan Stockdale

1797 Meadowdale Avenue
Atlanta, GA 30306
(404) 872-4434
(404) 815-2073 fax
Susan1797@aol.com

Susan Stockdale's author-illustrator program covers the children's picture book from creation to publication. Students learn about nonfiction writing and illustrating, amazing facts about animal behavior (the theme of Susan's books), and how hard work and persistence can help them achieve their dreams.

- Grade levels: 1-12

- $$

- *Nature's Paintbrush.* Simon & Schuster, 1999, ISBN 0689810814, Children's Book Council Outstanding Science Trade Book, Bank Street College of Education Citation for Excellence in Natural Science

  Some Sleep Standing Up. Simon & Schuster, 1996, ISBN 0689805098

Bettye Stroud

243 Deerhill Drive
Bogart, GA 30622
(706) 353-7290
(706) 552-3996 fax
Bstroud@webtv.net
<www.interkan.net/ravenstonepress/Bstroud.html>

Bettye Stroud's *Aim for the Stars* presentation includes a discussion of the writing life and a demonstration of how a book is made. Her props-and-paraphernalia bag contains fun gadgets that inspire enthusiastic reading and writing.

- Grade levels: K-6

- $

- *The World's Wide Open, a Collection of African American Poetry.* Simon & Schuster, 2003, ISBN 0689840268

  Dance Y'All. Marshall Cavendish, 2001, ISBN 0761450653

  The Leaving. Marshall Cavendish, 2001, ISBN 076145057x

- Requirements: Carousel slide projector, overhead projector

Illinois

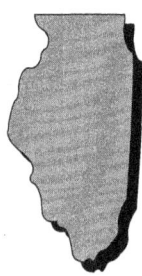

Mike Anderson

PO Box 35
Jacksonville, IL 62651
(217) 245-2207
mike@dulcimerguy.com
<www.dulcimerguy.com>

 Mike Anderson is a musician, a storyteller, an educator, and an author who uses skills from all of these disciplines in his workshops and presentations. As a folk musician, he plays guitar, old-time banjo, jaw harp, nose flute, bones, and a bunch of musical instruments made from junk. He's well known as a mountain dulcimer player, but also is an award-winning storyteller.

- Grade levels: K-12
- $$
- *The Phantom Teacher.* First Books Library, 2001, ISBN 0759620903
- *The Great Sled Race, Denny and I.* Volume 2, MW Productions, 2000, ISBN 1929050100, Parents' Choice Silver Honors
- Requirements: Sound system with two microphones

Pamela M. Anzalotti

761 Clarendon Lane
Aurora, IL 60504
(630) 375-1062
anzalottipm@Ameritech.net

Pamela Anzalotti offers students a chance to discover and explore natural science through art during her exciting slide show about scientific illustrators and their work. She brings specimens for students to observe, study, and draw with the help of step-by-step instructions. Topics include freaky fossils, tree treasures, water houses (shells), and mineral miracles. Pamela's also the instructor of the Magic Pencil Illustrator's Club and a lecturer on illustration topics, including covers, botanical illustration, fantasy illustration, and textbooks.

- Grade levels: K-12
- $
- Requirements: Slide projector, art supplies for students (list will be provided)

Franny Billingsley

5630 South Kimbark
Chicago, IL 60637
(773) 324-5637
rhpetten@midway.uchicago.edu
<www.frannybillingsley.com>

 Franny Billingsley's playful, interactive program focuses on building character, plot, and story. Her writing workshop uses props and metaphor games to enhance students' learning and inductive reasoning. Franny's lively exploration of the creative process and her rapport with students inspire them to look at writing in a new light.

- Grade levels: 3-8
- $$
- *The Folk Keeper.* Simon & Schuster/Atheneum, 1999, ISBN 0689828764, 0689844611 pbk, *Boston Globe*/Horn Book

Award for fiction, American Library Association Notable, Booklist Editor's Choice, *School Library Journal* Best Book, *Publishers Weekly* Best Book

Well Wished. Simon & Schuster/Atheneum, 1997, ISBN 0689812108, 0689832559 pbk, *School Library Journal* Best Book, Booklist Top Ten First Novels for Youth, *School Library Journal* Sleeper, Anne Spencer Lindbergh Prize Honor Book

Marlene Targ Brill

314 Lawndale
Wilmette, IL 60091
(847) 251-4448
mtbrill@worldnet.att.net

Join Marlene Brill in a research adventure to find exciting facts and writing tips during workshops such as *Searching for the Tooth Fairy, The Great Treasure Hunt,* and *From Tooth Fairies to Drummer Boy*s. She's also happy to share her very gross tooth collection with kids.

- Grade levels: 1-12

- $$

- *Margaret Knight: Girl Inventor.* Millbrook, 2001, ISBN 0761317562

  Tooth Tales from Around the World. Charlesbridge, 1998, ISBN 088163983, 088106391 pbk, International Reading Association/Children's Book Council Children's Choice Award

  Diary of a Drummer Boy. Millbrook, 1998, ISBN 0761301186

- Requirements: Slide projector, table

Phyllis Ann Burns

15805 Sharp Road
Carlyle, IL 62231
(618) 594-3378

Phyllis Burns tells students stories of what it was like to cross the prairie by wagon train on the Oregon Trail, sharing such details as the time she "saw" a cow drown, then saw a man swimming with chicken on his head.

- Grade levels: K-8

- $

David R. Collins

3403 45th Street
Moline, IL 61265
(309) 762-8985

David Collins was an English teacher for 30 years. Then, in 1970, he began writing books, mostly biographies, and has watched an impressive number of them (more than 80 at last count) march into print. He shares personal writing experiences and tips for improving student writing in his humorous presentations, which convey his "double E" standard: to entertain and educate. He recalls that some of his best childhood adventures were in books, adding that his writing career is a way for him to "pay back the favor."

- Grade levels: K-8

- $$

- *Ishi: The Last of His People.* With Kris Bergren, Morgan Reynolds, 2000, ISBN 188346544

  Tiger Woods, Golf Superstar. Pelican, 1999, ISBN 156554322X

Carolyn Crimi

1930 Orrington Avenue
Evanston, IL 60201
(847) 869-4043
(847) 492-0211 fax
crims@aol.com
<www.carolyncrimi.com>

Carolyn Crimi discusses her life as an author during her enthusiastic presentation, which emphasizes where she gets her ideas and shows students how to go on a story hunt for ideas, which are everywhere. She also uses props, including her 30-year-old teddy bear and her fifth grade diary.

- Grade levels: K-12

- $$

- *Tessa's Tip-tapping Toes.* Illustrated by Marsha Gray Carrington, Orchard, 2002, ISBN 0439317681

Kidding Around Chicago. Avon Travel, 2000, ISBN 1562615874

Don't Need Friends. Illustrated by Lynn Munsinger, Random House, 1999, ISBN 0385326432, Kentucky Bluegrass Award, Chicago Public Library Best of the Best, also in Spanish, French, and Korean editions

James Dague

18145 South Lawndale Avenue
Homewood, IL 60430
(708) 957-7822
(708) 957-5974 fax
<www.scribblebooks.com>

James Dague's *Fieldtrip That Comes to You* is an adventure in creativity designed to stimulate children's creative expression through music, dance, reading, and scribbling. His presentation on *What To Do Without TV* helps students discover creative alternatives to watching television. For special-needs kids, he offers *I'm Special: Celebrating Yourself* and *Differences*, which are designed to get them thinking positively about diversity.

- Grade levels: K-6
- $$
- *Scribble Monster and the Crunchy Crunchy Carrots.* Scribble Books, 2001, ISBN 0970640609

  Scribble Monster and the Broken TV. ScribbleBooks, 2001, ISBN 0970640617

  Scribble Monster Takes a Bath. ScribbleBooks, 2001, ISBN 0970640625

Brian "Fox" Ellis

PO Box 10800
Peoria, IL 61612
(309) 676-5223
foxtales@foxtalesint.com
<www.foxtalesint.com>

Since 1982, Fox Ellis has been traveling the world collecting and telling tales that help students make the connections between cultures and ecosystems, history and natural history. He teaches creative writing across the curriculum with an emphasis on linking poetry and nonfiction.

- Grade levels: K-12
- $$
- *Frog Songs: A Collection of Modern Haiku.* Foxtales International, 2000, no ISBN

  Learning from the Land: Teaching Ecology through Stories and Hands-on Science. Teacher Ideas Press, 1997, ISBN 1563085631

Judith Bloom Fradin

2121 Dobson Street
Evanston, IL 60202
(847) 869-8099
yudiff@aol.com

Judy Fradin shows students how her research techniques are basically the same as those kids use in school and explores how a nonfiction book evolves from an idea and how students might become writers. She's a skilled archival photographer who often collaborates on books with her husband, Dennis.

- Grade levels: K-12
- $$
- *Fight On: The Life of Mary Church Terrell.* Clarion, 2003, ISBN 0618133496

  Who Was Sacagawea? Penguin Putnam, 2002, ISBN 0448424851

  How Do You Say Grandma? Millbook, 2002, ISBN 0761324070

- Requirements: Slide projector

Kathleen Gibson

Aurora, IL 60504
(630) 585-7817
(630) 585-6809 fax
katgibson@aol.com
<www.kathleengibson.com>

Kathleen Gibson introduces students to basic song writing and poetry writing in *Rap Shop,* her presentation that uses the hottest sounds to help kids explore creative strategies by writing and recording rap songs. In her *Songs Are Stories, Too* program, students enjoy a concert of original, award-winning songs and stories. Kathleen also offers a keynote speech for adults, *For Our Children—Living Lives of Service*, to honor those who inspire us with selfless service to children's causes. Kathleen has won awards from Parents' Choice, given more than 1,500 live performances, and been featured on international TV and radio.

- Grade levels: K-8
- $$$
- *Zibber Bibber*. Rainbow Readers, 1996, ISBN 1888862009

   Free the Trees. Rainbow Readers, 1996, ISBN 188862017

   Rocking Chair Love. Rainbow Readers, 1996, ISBN 1888862025
- Requirements: Electricity

Linda Gorham

1009 Chadwick Court
Aurora, IL 60504-9470
(630) 851-9415
(630) 851-9404 fax
Lgorham2@aol.com
<www.storytelling.org/Gorham>

Linda Gorham's stories are fun, full of energy, and designed to enhance the joy of storytelling and students' love of reading. Her tales reinforce values, spark imaginations, and explore ideas and traditions from other cultures. She tells interactive African and multicultural folktales, inspirational stories, fables, "respect" stories, hero stories, Civil War tales, mythological love stories, and, of course, spooky stories.

- Grade levels: K-12
- $

Gene Gryniewicz

7509 West 161st Place
Tinley Park, IL 60477
(708) 532-8603
ggryn@hotmail.com
<www.tale-teller.com>
<happyfeetare.us-homepage.com>

Gene Gryniewicz tells folktales, both American and international, with voices, movements, characterizations, and an occasional pratfall. If he tells stories in tandem with his wife, he often includes dance, games, and crafts.

- Grade levels: K-12
- $$
- Requirements: Open space to move in, sound system

Leanne Johnson

544 Inca Boulevard
Carol Stream, IL 60188
(815) 979-9196
(630) 665-0108 fax (call first)
DayLeaG@aol.com
<www.storytelling.org/Leanne>

Leanne Johnson combines her love for music with her passion for storytelling to bring new life to old and original tales, including international folktales, scary stories, poetry, and songs. Her stories are sprinkled with touches of Celtic harp, tin whistle, or bodhran.

- Grade levels: K-12
- $
- Requirements: Wireless microphone, small table, high stool

Anna M. Johnson-Webb (Momma Kemba)

5521 West Walton Street
Chicago, IL 60651
(773) 287-1336
(773) 287-0170 fax
Kembawebb@aol.com
<www.storytelling.org/kemba>

Momma Kemba travels the U.S. and abroad keeping alive the spirit of strong black women in American history through drama and song. Her presentations are done in full costume and are rich in a cappella spirituals and audience participation. Characters Momma Kemba offers to bring alive include Dr. Mary Jane McLeod Bethune, Harriet Tubman, Sojourner Truth, Ida B. Wells, Aunt Clara Brown, and Fannie Lou Hamer.

- Grade levels: 3-12
- $
- Requirements: Lavalier microphone, chair, podium

Marilyn A. Kinsella

645 Pleasant Ridge Road
Fairview Heights, IL 62208
(618) 397-1377
markinsella19@hotmail.com
<communities.msn.com/TaleypoTales>

Marilyn Kinsella's collection of more than 100 stories includes folktales; personal stories about growing up in Southern Illinois; and literary, original, and historical tales. She has vast experience telling tales in every setting from nursery schools to nursing homes, and is the storyteller at the Edwardsville Public Library.

- Grade levels: K-8
- $
- *Taleypo Tales.* Cassette, self-published, no ISBN

Patricia K. Kummer

2671 Normandy Place
Lisle, IL 60532
(630) 355-2219
patriciakummer@netscape.net
<www.scbwi-illinois.org/Kummer.html>

Patricia Kummer's presentation on how writers work features materials from her own projects, which she uses to help students explore research and interviewing methods. In her talk on how writers' words become books, she presents an overview of the publishing process and highlights career opportunities.

- Grade levels: 3-8
- $$
- *Ukraine.* Children's Press, 2001, ISBN 0516211013

  Alabama. Capstone Press, 1998, ISBN 1560654996, Chicago Women in Publishing Award, Illinois Women's Press Association Award for juvenile nonfiction

  Cote d'Ivoire. Children's Press, 1996, ISBN 0516026410, Chicago Women in Publishing Award for Juvenile Tradebooks 1997
- Requirements: Slide projector, overhead projector

Kevin Luthardt

8936 North Lamon, #3
Skokie, IL 60077
(847) 674-5429 phone/fax
luthardt@juno.com

Kevin Luthardt's interactive presentation takes students through the process of how a picture book is created and gives them an up-close look at artwork from his book, including preliminary sketches, the original manuscript, and the final oil paintings. He also teaches students simple drawing techniques and helps them create storyboards for their own picture books.

- Grade levels: 1-6
- $
- *Peep!* Peachtree, 2003, ISBN 156145046

  Mine. Simon & Schuster/Atheneum, 2001, ISBN 0689832370
- Requirements: Easel, small table, dry-erase board

Paddy Lynn

212 East Walker Place
Mundelein, IL 60060
(847) 566-6391
paddytale@aol.com
<www.storytelling.org/paddylynn>

Using costume pieces and props, Paddy Lynn gives programs of stories from around the world or of thrilling, spine-tingling chillers. Students can also enjoy his *Peace Pipe* tales, which are a combination of Native American myths and legends, or tales from the Oregon Trail, which depict one woman's family's adventures.

- Grade levels: K-4
- $-$$$

Lisa Mallen

2203 Caledonia Court
Naperville, IL 60564
(630) 922-4488
(630) 922-4489 fax
LRMallen@wideopenwest.com

Lisa Mallen shares her journey to being an author, which began when, as a mother of three, she discovered that she didn't want to just read lots of children's books: She wanted to write them, too. Now that she's an author, she visits schools and talks about reading, writing, and following your dreams.

- Grade levels: K-5
- $
- *Elton the Elf.* Lobster Press, 2001, ISBN 1894222334, Alcuin Book Award
- Requirements: Dry-erase board, markers

Maryjane Miller

21 Spinning Wheel Road, #11-D
Hinsdale, IL 60521
(630) 986-9324
JMMJ39@aol.com

Discover where writing hides—in our imaginations, in memory, in questions—with Maryjane's presentation as she shares the story of how her book, *Me and My Name,* answered many questions. Words took Dorothy to Oz and are like a basket, woven piece by piece. Learn how writing hides in those words.

- Grade levels: K-6
- $$
- *Me and My Name.* iUniverse, 2001 (originally Penguin), now out-of-print, ISBN 0685043467

   Upside Down. iUniverse, 2000 (originally Viking, 1992), ISBN 05953467

   Fast Forward. iUniverse, 2000 (originally Viking 1993), ISBN 0595003338

Patricia Hruby Powell

675N CR 1375E
Tuscola, IL 61953
(217) 253-3292 phone/fax (at tone, press *51)
phpowell@talesforallages.com
<www.talesforallages.com>
<www.scbwi-illinois.org/Powell>

Patricia Powell traveled internationally as a dancer who told stories; now she travels as a storyteller who dances and uses percussion instruments from around the world in her performances. Patricia also offers *An Evening (Morning or Afternoon) with Jane Austen, Emily Bronte and Emily Dickinson,* a program in costume with props, for high schoolers and adults. Funding through the Illinois Arts Council is possible for schools in Illinois.

- Grade levels: K-12
- $$
- *Zinnia: A Navajo Bilingual Story.* Salina Bookshelf, 2003, forthcoming

   Blossom Tales: Flower Stories of Many Folk. Illustrated by Sarah Dillard, Moon Mountain Publishing, 2002, ISBN 0967792983

   Mothers, Daughters, Sisters, Grandmothers. Cassette, self-published, Creative Arts Institute Award

- Requirements: Sound system, microphone on pole stand or cordless microphone

Dan Robbins

19 W 030 Normany East
Oak Brook, IL 60523
(630) 963-3732
(630) 241-4558 fax
robbinspbn@earthlink.net
<danrobbinspaintbynumbersguru.com>

You look, but what do you see? Dan Robbins tells the story of Arty, a youngster who wants to become a real artist, and his encounter with the Wizard of Paint-by-Numbers. The wizard tells Arty that if he pays attention as he paints by numbers, the process can become an artistic learning experience. Students are given paint-by-number sets or assignments so they can "see for themselves." Dan tells students what it took to bring a simple idea like paint-by-numbers from near failure to being enshrined, 50 years later, in the Smithsonian as part of our cultural heritage. This story is accompanied by a slide show of illustrations and read-along text.

- Grade levels: 4-8, adult
- $
- *Bigger Than It Looks.* Possum Hill Press, 1997, ISBN 096606934X

Mary Ellyn Sandford

4507 Chelsea Avenue
Lisle, IL 60532
(630) 963-5554
wfkig@quixnet.net

Mary Ellyn Sandford speaks to students about how to get started writing, how to rewrite, and how to submit material to publishers, then provides hands-on opportunities to practice writing.

- Grade levels: K-12
- $
- Requirements: Overhead projector or setup for PowerPoint

Barbara Santucci

10852 Whispering Pines Way
Rockford, IL 61114
(815) 885-3695
(815) 885-3352 fax
bgsantucci@juno.com

Barbara Santucci offers interactive classroom presentations, including *Journaling Your Memories,* which focuses on writing a short piece and creating a "memory journal" of words, pictures, mementos, and letters. *Capture Those Details* shows students how to write a descriptive piece about an object picked from her "secret" box. *Stories and Poems from Paintings* uses famous artists' work, while her slide show on *Loon Summer* includes a story and art activity about loons.

- Grade levels: K-6
- $
- *Abby's Chair.* Eerdmans, 2003, forthcoming

  Anna's Corn. Eerdmans, 2002, ISBN 0802851193

  Loon Summer. Eerdmans, 2001, ISBN 0802851827

Megan Wells

427 North Brainard Avenue
La Grange Park, IL 60526
(708) 352-2631
meganwells@juno.com
<www.storytelling.org>

Renowned for her passion and mythic style, Megan Wells appears at storytelling venues around the country. She draws from a wide repertoire that includes Greek, Nordic, and multicultural myths; Chicago, American, and world history; legends; ghost stories; teaching tales; and original tales of beauty and insight. She's won two national storytelling awards: the EdPress Distinguished Achievement Award and the Parents' Choice Gold from *Parents Magazine.*

- Grade levels: K-12
- $$-$$$$

Cheryl Aylward Whitesel

5313 Grand Avenue
Western Springs, IL 60558
(708) 246-5394
(708) 246-5474 fax
caylwardw@yahoo.com

In her presentation on *Vanishing Tibet,* Cheryl Whitesel uses photos of Tibetan life and an array of Tibetan objects that students can see and touch to help them understand various aspects of Tibetan life, such as schooling, nomadism, Buddhism, and the Chinese occupation. She also offers a workshop on how to become an author and how ideas are transformed into books, during which she shows students illustrations from her childhood and discusses with them her adult efforts to become a published author.

- Grade levels: 4-12
- $
- *Rebel: A Tibetan Odyssey.* HarperCollins, 2000, ISBN 0688167357, New York Public Library Books for the Teen Age, Junior Library Guild Selection, Notable Social Studies trade book
- Requirements: Overhead projector

Indiana

Sharon Kirk Clifton

(812) 346-2072
magicbeans4you@hotmail.com
<groups.msn.com/SharonKirkCliftonStory-teller>

Sharon Clifton is an energetic, interactive, traditional storyteller whose well-crafted tales transport listeners of all ages into the world of imagination. In the character and attire of *Jack's Mama*, her signature program, she tells tales from the Appalachian oral tradition, giving insights into early settlers' lives. She's a recipient of the Lilly Teacher Creativity Fellowship Grant, among other awards, and a featured teller for the Indiana Cultural Arts program.

- Grade levels: K-12
- $-$$
- Requirements: Microphone

Hank Fincken

6303 Evanston Avenue
Indianapolis, IN 46220
(317) 255-3566 phone/fax
fincken@indy.net

Hank Fincken's National Theater Company of One performs original, one-man plays about Johnny Appleseed, Christopher Columbus, Thomas Edison, Francisco Pizarro, and a 49er on the California Trail. Scholars have checked the accuracy of the plays, and various arts and humanities organizations have endorsed them. Hank's been named a master artist by the Indiana Arts Commission and cited for his achievement and service by the Indiana Theatre Association.

- Grade levels: K-12
- $-$$$
- *Three Midwest History Plays and Then Some.* Guild Press of Indiana, 1998, no ISBN

Helen Frost

6108 Old Brook Drive
Fort Wayne, IN 46835
(219) 485-1785
frost-thompson@att.net
<www.helenfrost.com>

Helen Frost shares her love of writing with students and offers a wealth of writing ideas for reluctant writers, making them feel safe enough to make their voices heard. She uses narrative poems, oral tradition, and readings from her books to encourage and inspire young writers. She's written more than 90 nonfiction books for early readers and award-winning poetry for all ages, and she teaches an ongoing, collaborative, violence-prevention program with artists and musicians in her community.

- Grade levels: K-12
- $$
- *Keesha's House.* Farrar, Straus & Giroux/Frances Foster Books, 2003, ISBN 03743406411

German Immigrants: Coming to America Series. Capstone Press/Blue Earth Books, 2001, ISBN 0736807942

When I Whisper, Nobody Listens: Helping Young People Write About Difficult Issues. Heinemann, 2001, ISBN 0325003521

Florrie Binford Kichler

3842 Wolf Creek Circle
Carmel, IN 46033
(317) 844-6070
(317) 844-8935 fax
fkichler@patriapress.com

- What does a book author do? How does an illustrator decide what to draw? Where does a book cover come from? Florrie Kichler leads kids on a lively journey through the world of book publishing, using examples from her books and e-books.

- Grade levels: 3-5
- $
- *Juliette Low, Girl Scout Founder.* Patria Press, 2002, ISBN 1882859081

  William Henry Harrison, Young Tippecanoe. Patria Press, 2000, ISBN 1882859030

  Amelia Earhart, Young Air Pioneer. Patria Press, 1999, ISBN 1882859022

- Requirements: Overhead projector

Elsa Marston

1926 Dexter Street
Bloomington, IN 47401
(812) 332-3881
harik@indiana.edu

- Why go to the fuss and bother of taking your class to Egypt when you can bring Elsa Marston to your class to talk about mummies and ancient worlds? She also enjoys discussing writing, hatching a plot, grabbing an idea, and what "imagination" really means. Her books and presentations explore the here-and-now, as well as long ago-and-faraway, and are designed to spark kids' eagerness to learn more about our world.

- Grade levels: 3-12
- $$
- *The Phoenicians.* Marshall Cavendish, 2001, ISBN 0761403094

  Women in the Middle East: Tradition and Change. Franklin Watts, 1996, New York Public Library Books for the Teen Age

  The Fox Maiden. Simon & Schuster, 1996, ISBN 0689801076, Bank Street College Best Children's Books of the Year

April Pulley Sayre

17912 Edgewood Walk
South Bend, IN 46635
(219) 277-5475
apsayre@aol.com
<www.aprilsayre.com>

- A sense of wonder and a little wackiness are the trademarks of April Sayre's recounting of her adventures researching dozens of books about nature and rain forests. She plays tapes of animal noises, teaches kids animal calls, and talks about the process of writing. She offers a session called *Put On Some Antlers and Walk Like a Moose,* which teaches kids to find, follow, and study wild animals, and one called *Writing Wild!*

- Grade levels: K-8
- $$
- *The Army Ant Parade.* Henry Holt, 2002, ISBN 0805063536

  Noodle Man: The Past Superhero. Orchard Books, 2002, ISBN 0439293073

  Dig, Wait, Listen: A Desert Toad's Tale. Greenwillow, 2001, ISBN 0688166156

- Requirements: Slide projector, tape player, microphone

Peter J. Welling

8051 Cardinal Cove East
Indianapolis, IN 46256
(317) 577-8109
(317) 594-8389 fax
aldertag@comcast.net
<www.peterwelling.com>

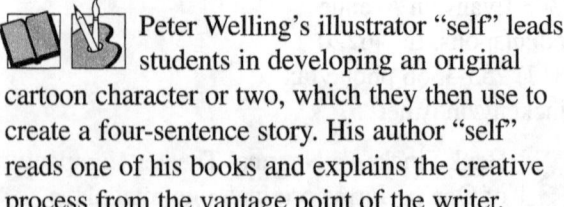 Peter Welling's illustrator "self" leads students in developing an original cartoon character or two, which they then use to create a four-sentence story. His author "self" reads one of his books and explains the creative process from the vantage point of the writer.

- Grade levels: K-5
- $
- *Shawn O'Hisser, the Last Snake in Ireland.* Pelican, 2002, ISBN 1589800141

  Andrew McGroundhog and His Shady Shadow. Pelican, 2000, ISBN 156554711x

- Requirements: White-paper flip chart, easel

Kentucky

Roberta Simpson Brown

PO Box 43745
Louisville, KY 40253-0745
(502) 244-1291 phone/fax

Roberta Brown specializes in scary stories that help people face their fears and learn to deal with them. In her workshops, she encourages participants to share stories about, confront, and live with whatever scares them, and promotes interest in writing, reading, and language.

- Grade levels: 5-12
- $-$$
- *Scared in School.* August House, 1997, ISBN 0874834961

  Queen of the Cold-Blooded Tales. August House, 1993, ISBN 0874833329

  The Walking Trees and Other Scary Stories. August House, 1991, ISBN 0874831431
- Requirements: Microphone

Marcia Thornton Jones

1085 Deer Crossing Way
Lexington, KY 40509
(859) 263-2512
marciajones@att.net
<www.Baileykids.com>
<www.Barkleyschool.com>

As a best-selling author and award-winning teacher, Marcia Jones inspires writers of all ages to use the writing process successfully. During her lively presentations, students learn a five-step writing process while brainstorming ideas, developing characters, and drafting stories. Marcia encourages audiences young and old to make writing a part of their everyday lives. She's the author of more than 86 titles and four best-selling series, including *Bailey School Kids, Barkley's School for Dogs,* and *Triplet Trouble.*

- Grade levels: 1-5
- $$$
- Requirements: Overhead projector, microphone

Pat Mora

2925 Sequoia Drive
Edgewood, KY 41017
<www.patmora.com>

Pat Mora is committed to sharing book joy with English- and Spanish-speaking people of all ages through readings from her work, a slide show on her sources of inspiration, and hints on the writing process. This award-winning author of books for adults and children engages her audiences in exploring practices that strengthen writing, fosters respect for languages, and stresses the importance of reading for writers.

- Grade levels: 2-12
- $$$$
- *My Own True Name: New and Selected Poems for Young Adult.* Piñata/Arte Publico Press, 2000, ISBN 1558852921, New York Public Library Recommended Books for the Teen Age

This Big Sky. Scholastic, 1998, ISBN 0590371207, Texas Institute of Letters Award for Best Book for Children/Young People, American Library Association Notable, PEN Center West finalist, New York Public Library 100 Books for Reading and Sharing

Tomas and the Library Lady. Knopf, 1997, ISBN 0679804019 (available in Spanish), Bluebonnet Master List, International Reading Association Teacher's Choice, Tomas Rivera Mexican American Children's Book Award

■ Requirements: Slide projector, podium, lapel microphone

Maine

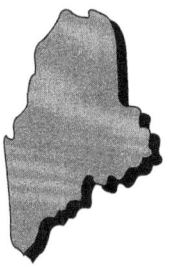

Robert F. Baldwin

PO Box 41
Newcastle, ME 04553
(207) 586-6069
storytlr@tidewater.net
<geocities.com/storytlr_2000/author_page.html>

Bob Baldwin has spent most of his life as a writer, folksinger, and storyteller, and he loves showing children how songs, poetry, fiction, and even nonfiction can powerfully convey knowledge, feelings, and images.

- Grade levels: K-6
- $$
- *Cities Through Time: Beijing.* Lerner, 1999, ISBN 082253214x

  This Is the Sea That Feeds Us. Dawn Publications, 1998, ISBN 1883220696, International Reading Association Teacher's Choice

  New England Whaler. Lerner, 1996, ISBN 0822529785
- Requirements: Table

Toni Buzzeo

59 Back Nippen Road
Buxton, ME 04093
tonibuzzeo@tonibuzzeo.com
<www.tonibuzzeo.com>

How do we know what really happened long ago? Can we distinguish between fact and legend? In the spirit of historical inquiry, Toni Buzzeo entices students to discover the importance of historical research and the value of family stories. She shares her own story, from shy child to published author and all of the stops between.

- Grade levels: K-6
- $
- *Dawdle Duckling.* Illustrated by Margaret Spengler, Dial, 2003, ISBN 0803727313

  The Sea Chest. Illustrated by Mary GrandPre, Dial, 2002, ISBN 0803727038

  Terrific Connections with Authors, Illustrators and Storytellers: Real Space and Virtual Links with Authors, Illustrators and Storytellers. With Jane Kurtz, Libraries Unlimited, 1999, ISBN 1563087448
- Requirements: Overhead projector, screen, easel, chart paper

Robert Davidson

PO Box 125
York Beach, ME 03910
(207) 351-1185
redbob@gwi.net

Robert Davidson's presentation for parents is primarily for schools, hospitals, and community education programs. In it, he shares interviews he's done with successful parents around the country who were recommended to him by high school principals because their children are socially and academically well-rounded, competent, and happy.

- Grade levels: Parents and educators of K-12
- $$
- *How Good Parents Raise Great Kids: The Six Essential Habits of Highly Successful Parents,* Warner, 1996, ISBN 0446671371

Jennifer Richard Jacobson

PO Box 127
Cumberland, ME 04021
(207) 829-5234 phone/fax
Jennifer@jenniferjacobson.com
<www.jenniferjacobson.com>

Through lively storytelling accompanied by visuals and props, young children learn how Jennifer Jacobson's life experiences sneak their way into her writing. Jennifer also reveals how she creates characters that readers can care about and what she's learned about plot structure. Using picture books and old-fashioned melodrama, she demonstrates how authors use the "rule of three" to plot successful stories.

- Grade levels: K-5
- $-$$
- *I Don't Want to Go to School.* Candlewick, 2003, ISBN 0807540714

  Winnie Dancing on Her Own. Houghton Mifflin, 2001, ISBN 0618132872, Top Ten First Novel 2001, Junior Library Guild selection

  Moon Sandwich Mom. Albert Whitman, 1999, ISBN 0807540714

- Requirements: Overhead projector, chart paper, easel

David Lint as "Dafydd the Storyteller"

196 Park Street
Orono, ME 04473
(207) 866-3473
Dlint@maine.edu
<www.storyteller.net>

When Dafydd the Storyteller walks into a room playing his Irish drum, kids know that magic is about to happen. Audiences are drawn into a time of magic, love, and courage through the power of story in the Irish tradition, which Dafydd learned from his grandfather.

- Grade levels: K-12
- $

Sharon L. Lovejoy

PO Box 249
South Bristol, ME 04568-0249
(207) 644-1712
(207) 644-1713 fax
Sharon@sharonlovejoy.com
<www.sharonlovejoy.com>

Sharon Lovejoy is an experienced gardener and naturalist with an extensive background in natural history, ethnobotany, herbs, nature crafts, and garden design. She's also an expert on children's gardening and has been a guest on numerous TV and radio shows, as well as being a contributing editor for *Country Living Gardener.*

- Grade levels: Prefers to speak to adults who work with children
- $$
- *Sunflower Houses: Inspiration from the Garden,* Workman, 2001, ISBN 0761123865

  Roots, Shoots, Buckets and Boots: Gardening Together with Children. Workman, 1999, ISBN 0761117652, 0761110569 pbk

  Hollyhock Days: Garden Adventures for the Young at Heart. Interweave Press, 1998, ISBN 1883010012, 0934026904 pbk

- Requirements: Slide projector, clip-on microphone

Amy MacDonald

10 Winslow Road
Falmouth, ME 04105
(207) 781-5526
(207) 781-5223 fax
AmyMac@maine.rr.com
<www.AmyMacDonald.com>

Amy MacDonald examines sources of creativity by doing a quick writing exercise in which students come up with new ideas for stories. She also speaks about the many pleasures and pitfalls of writing, including editing and revision. With very young students, she creates a Big Book based on rhyme. Her *Writing by Storm* workshop, developed through the Kennedy Center for the Performing Arts, teaches students to use brainstorming to produce a finished story; this method can empower even the most reluctant writer.

- Grade levels: K-6
- $$-$$$
- *No More Nice.* Farrar, Straus & Giroux, 1996, ISBN 0531095428, Parents' Choice

  Little Beaver and the Echo. Putnam, 1990, ISBN 0698116283, Silver Stylus Award, Children's Book Award, Kate Greenaway Award, *New York Times* Best Books of 1990, *The Independent* United Kingdom Best Books of the Century

  Rachel Fister's Blister. Houghton Mifflin, 1990, ISBN 0395521521, International Reading Association/Children's Book Council Children's Choice, Horn Book Fanfare Best of 1990
- Requirements: Slide projector, microphone, overhead projector, blackboard, easel

Bruce McMillan

176 County Road
PO Box 85
Shapleigh, ME 04076-0085
(207) 324-9453
brucie@cybertours.com
<www.brucemcmillan.com>

 Bruce McMillan's enthusiasm for the writing profession is highly contagious. A writer, photo-illustrator, and teacher of writing, Bruce travels widely to conferences, libraries, and schools to share his love of books, writing, and reading through slide shows, talks, and sharing. He has more than 40 books currently in print and has won numerous awards for his nonfiction titles.

- Grade levels: K-12
- $$$
- *Day of the Ducklings.* Houghton Mifflin, 2001, ISBN 0618048782

  Nights of the Pufflings. Houghton Mifflin, 1995, ISBN 0395708109

  Mouse Views: What the Class Pet Saw. Holiday House, 1993, ISBN 0823410080

Tammy Packie

PO Box 117
Hulls Cove, ME 04644
(207) 288-5442
tpackie@downeast.net
<www.downeast.net/tpackiephoto>

Photographer and teacher Tammy Packie enjoys sharing with students basic photographic skills, her appreciation of historical and contemporary photography, and, especially, black-and-white processing techniques. She prefers working with kids who have access to cameras.

- Grade levels: 1-12
- $
- *Photographing Maine, 1840-2000.* Center for Maine Contemporary Art, 2000, no ISBN

Learnin' Vernon

PO Box 198
Howland, ME 04448
(207) 759-6089
LearninVernon@yahoo.com

Storyteller and motivational speaker Vernon tells legends from faraway lands, tales from Maine folklore, and stories to lift the spirit.

- Grade levels: K-12
- $
- Requirements: Wireless microphone

Maryland

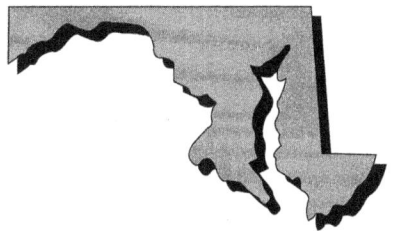

Fred Bowen

9104 Warren Street
Silver Spring, MD 20910
(301) 585-0288
(301) 585-2932 fax (call first)
Sportstory@aol.com
<www.fredbowen.com>

📖 Fred Bowen, author of nine children's sports novels and a *Washington Post* sports columnist for kids, engages his audiences with interesting and often funny stories about his life as a sportswriter, while inspiring students with tips on how to make their own writing better. He shares with adults his secrets for getting sports-crazy kids to love reading and challenges the perception that sports is a narrow interest, stressing its great drama and the power of good sports writing to capture that drama.

- Grade levels: 3-5
- $$
- *Full Court Fever.* Peachtree, 1998, ISBN 1561451606, Maryland Children's Book Award

  T. J.'s Secret Pitch. Peachtree, 1996, ISBN 1561451193, Family Channel Seal of Quality

Ellen Butts

4523 Dorset Avenue
Chevy Chase, MD 20815
(301) 652-2454
ellenbutts@hotmail.com

📖 In collaboration with cowriter Joyce Schwartz, Ellen Butts offers students insight into how a book is created by using examples from her biography projects. Students are asked to choose someone they know and to jot down information about them, then use those notes to write an opening paragraph that will make readers want to know more about their subject.

- Grade levels: 3-8
- $$
- *Eugenie Clark: Adventures of a Shark Scientist.* Linnet Books, 2000, ISBN 0208024409

  Carl Sagan. Lerner, 2000, ISBN 0822549867

  May Chinn: The Best Medicine. Scientific American Books for Young Readers, 1995, ISBN 0716765896, 071676590 pbk, Women's National Book Association Books for 21st Century Girls
- Requirements: Easel, large pad of lined paper

Priscilla Cummings

3026 Aberdeen Road
Annapolis, MD 21403
(410) 269-7591
(410) 295-0922 fax
priscummings@comcast.net
<www.childrensbookguild.org/priscillacummings.html>

📖 Priscilla Cummings talks with kids about how she combines fact and fiction to create the *Chadwick the Crab* series and shows them how a book is put together, from coming up with the idea to rewriting and re-rewriting. She received the Metro Washington Association for

Maryland 49

Childhood Education International Literary Award in 2001 for her nine picture books about the Chesapeake Bay.

- Grade levels: K-8

- $

- *A Face First.* Dutton, 2001, ISBN 0525465227, *School Library Journal* starred review

  Autumn Journey. Dutton, 1997, ISBN 0525652388, American Booksellers Association Pick of the List, Maryland Black-eyed Susan Shortlist

  Chadwick the Crab. Tidewater Publishers, 1986, ISBN 087033347x

- Requirements: Overhead projector, screen

Edward Allan Faine

PO Box 5346
Takoma Park, MD 20913
(301) 587-1202
efaine@yahoo.com
<www.takoma.com/ned/home.htm>

In his school visits, Edward Faine talks about how to make a book, using specific examples from his own work and showing students drafts of pictures, text, and more. He also talks to older students about the history of the book and discusses the writing process.

- Grade levels: K-12

- $

- *The Balloon Galloon.* Illustrated by Joan C. Waites, IM Press 2001, ISBN 0965465187

  Ned Ventures: Teenage Life in the '50s. IM Press, 2001, ISBN 0965465179

  Little Ned Stories. Illustrated by Joan C. Waite, IM Press, 1999, ISBN 0965465152

Carla Golembe

11215 Oak Leaf Drive, #1210
Silver Spring, MD 20901
(301) 754-1579
(301) 754-3968 fax
Cyber2lip@aol.com
<www.addcenter.net/Carla/Carla.html>

Carla Golembe's presentation includes a brief talk, drawing demonstration, and discussion of the various steps involved in writing and illustrating a children's book, including where ideas come from. The drawing demonstration allows children to see an artist in action. Throughout the presentation, she stresses the importance of individual creative expression, the revision of ideas and images, and the many sources from which one can derive ideas.

- Grade levels: 1-12

- $

- *Honeybees.* By Deborah Heiligman, National Geographic Society, 2002, ISBN 0792266781

  Washington DC ABC's. VSP Books, 2001, ISBN 1893622061

  Dog Magic. Houghton Mifflin, 1997, ISBN 0395816629

- Requirements: Easel, table

Michelle Y. Green

14118 Rev. Rainsford Court
Upper Marlboro, MD 20772
(301) 574-4947
(301) 574-1095 fax
Mgreen5@bellatlantic.net
<www.williepearl.com>

Michelle Green's school visits feature her insights on the writing life, including what it's really like, where ideas come from, and how characters come alive. She also offers sessions on writing family stories using archival photos and artifacts, and speaks about the process of getting published, including dealing with agents, contracts, and marketing.

- Grade levels: 4-12

- $

- *A Strong Right Arm: The Story of Mamie "Peanut" Johnson.* Dial, 2002, ISBN 0803726619

  Willie Pearl: Under the Mountain. William Ruth & Co, 1992, ISBN 0962769711, Multicultural Publishers Exchange 1993 Children's Book of the Year (series won CRABbery Award for historical fiction)

Margaret Meacham

PO Box 402
Brooklandville, MD 21022
(410) 337-0736
(410) 337-9408 fax
mmeac@aol.com
<www.childrensbookguild.org/meacham>

Margaret Meacham discusses the writing process, how to get ideas for stories, research, how a book is made, and tips for young writers, but leaves plenty of time for questions. She's taught writing at Goucher College for 10 years and is the author of 12 books for children and young adults.

- Grade levels: 3-12

- $

- *Quiet! You're Invisible.* Holiday House, 2001, ISBN 0823416518

  Oyster Moon. Tidewater Publishers, 1996, ISBN 087033459x

  Secret of the Heron Creek. Tidewater, 1991, ISBN 087033414x

Joyce Schwartz

106 Hesketh Street
Chevy Chase, MD 20815
(301) 656-0946
jr.Schwartz@verizon.net

In collaboration with cowriter Ellen Butts, Joyce Schwartz offers students insight into how a book is created by using examples from her biography projects. Students are asked to choose someone they know and to jot down information about them, then use those notes to write an opening paragraph that will make readers want to know more about their subject.

- Grade levels: 3-8

- $$

- *Eugenie Clark: Adventures of a Shark Scientist.* Linnet Books, 2000, ISBN 0208024409

  Carl Sagan. Lerner, 2000, ISBN 0822549867

  May Chinn: The Best Medicine. Scientific American, 1995, ISBN 0716765896, 071676590 pbk, Women's National Book Association Books for 21st Century Girls

- Requirements: Easel, large pad of lined paper

Joseph Slate

15107 Interlachen Drive, #701
Silver Spring, MD 20906
joeslate@bellatlantic.net
<www.josephslate.com>

Joseph Slate says that even though he's approximately 203 years old, he gives talks and autographings at schools and libraries if the events are associated with large bookstore sponsorship, but he prefers discussing his *Miss Bindergarten* books at reading conferences and teacher events.

- Grade levels: K-12 (see note above)

- $$

Peggy Thomson

23 Grafton Street
Chevy Chase, MD 20815
(301) 656-3630
JSTsyc@aol.com
<www.childrensbookguild.org>

In Peggy Thomson's presentation, students learn about the fun of research—how to snoop in museums, zoos, or a spaghetti factory; how to tag along with a Navajo sheepherder; and how to train a museum guard dog or bathe an elephant. Her current research is teaching her how to communicate with orangutans using computer-generated, symbolic language! Peggy is a winner of the *Boston Globe* Horn Book Nonfiction Award, and one of her books won the National Science Teacher's Association/Children's Book Council outstanding science trade book for children award.

- Grade levels: 3-8

- $

- *Take Me Out to the Bat and Ball Factory.* Albert Whitman, 1998, ISBN 0807577375

  The Nine-ton Cat: Behind the Scenes at an Art Museum. Houghton Mifflin, 1997, ISBN 0395826551, 0395826837 pbk

  Siggy's Spaghetti Works. Tambourine, 1993, ISBN 0688113737, 0688113745 pbk

Massachusetts

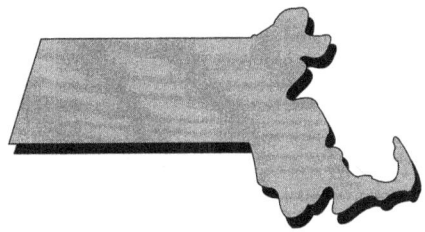

Monica Driscoll Beatty

527 School Street
Belmont, MA 02478
(617) 484-3637
monicabeatty@mindspring.com
<www.author-illustr-source.com/monicabeatty.htm>

Monica Beatty's presentation on the writing process includes discussion of writing, research, revision, editing, illustration, paste-ups, and dummies, as well as finding and working with a publisher. She also reads from her books and discusses hospitalization, surgery, looking and feeling different, tolerance and understanding, and personal safety.

- Grade levels: K-4

- $

- *Fire Night.* Health Press, 1999, ISBN 0929173317

  My Sister Rose Has Diabetes. Health Press, 1997, ISBN 0929173279, American Medical Writers Association Will Solimene Award

  Blueberry Eyes. Health Press, 1996, ISBN 0929173242, American Medical Writers Association Will Solimene Award for Excellence in Medical Communication

Judith Black

33 Prospect Street
Marblehead, MA 01945
(781) 631-4417
jb@storiesalive.com
<www.storiesalive.com>

Judith Black tells original tales from American history, as well as original stories and folktales that connect listeners to cultures and experiences that may transform their lives. Her renowned performances for adults include the fervent message that storytelling is a key to literacy. Judith has won storytelling awards from Parents' Choice, *Boston Parents Paper,* and numerous other organizations. She was commissioned by the U.S. Dept. of the Interior, NPR, and the Foundation for the Humanities to produce *The Home Front,* the story of women who built M-1 rifles at Springfield Armory during WWII. She also does a Chautauqua-style performance of Lucy Stone, whose powerful oratory and example turned national sentiment to abolition and women's rights 150 years ago.

- Grade levels: K-12

- $$$

- *Blooming: Stories for Girls to Grow On.* Tidal Wave Productions, 2001, ISBN 0970107315 cassette, 0970107307 CD, *Storytelling World* Honor Award, Parents' Choice Award, Pegasus awards for middle and high school

  Bringing the Story Home: The Complete Guide to Storytelling for Parents. Norton, 2000, ISBN 0393322602

  From Her Arms to His: Women on the 3rd Front during WWII. J&J Productions/CT Valley Historic Society, 1996, no ISBN, video, Cable Ace Award, Emmy nominee

Claire H. Blatchford

286 Patten Hill Road
Shelburne, MA 01370
(413) 625-8624 phone/fax
Edclaireb@aol.com

Claire Blatchford became deaf at age six from the mumps. Most of her writing is concerned with the "other door" that can open when the door to normal hearing closes. She shares her experiences of hearing through the eyes, hands, feet, and the "ear in the heart." She discusses face-reading, use of assistive hearing devices such as TTY and closed captioning, and, of course, writing. Her aim is to show kids that, deaf or not, reading and writing also can enable one to go out the "other door" into the great world all around and within.

- Grade levels: K-12
- $$$
- *Nick's Secret.* Lerner, 2000, ISBN 0822507439

  Going with the Flow. Carolrhoda, 1998, ISBN 1565052849

  Nick's Mission. Lerner, 1995, ISBN 0822507404

Pat Lowery Collins

3 Wauketa Road
Gloucester, MA 01930-1423
(978) 283-2749 phone/fax
patlc@earthlink.net
<www.author-illustr-source.com>
<www.authorsden.com>

 Pat Collins' most popular presentations are *I Am an Artist and So Are You* (based on her book) and *Find the Poet*. Each topic introduces students to all aspects of writing. She also offers a presentation on the development of her in-process picture book, *Schooner,* from photographs she took on site to creating the paintings in her studio.

- Grade levels: K-9
- $$
- *Just Imagine.* Houghton Mifflin, 2001, ISBN 0618056033

  Signs Wonders. Houghton Mifflin, 1999, ISBN 0395971195, New York Public Library Books for the Teen Age, Children's Literature Choice

  I Am an Artist. Millbrook, 1992, ISBN 156294729x

Jacqueline Davies

81 Parish Road
Needham, MA 02494
(781) 455-8334
(781) 455-8284 fax
jackiedavies@mediaone.net
<www.jacquelinedavies.net>

Regardless of her students' ages, Jacqueline Davies strives for one thing: to have each kid look in a mirror and see a writer. She wants kids to discover how much fun writing can be and offers workshops such as *Imagine That...*, which sparks creativity; *A Poem Is Not a Fish,* which teaches metaphor, anti-metaphor, and description; or *Three Truths and a Lie—Historical Fiction.* She's the 1998 winner of the Society of Children's Book Writers and Illustrators General Work-in-progress Award

- Grade levels: K-12
- $$
- *The Boy Who Drew Birds,* Houghton Mifflin, forthcoming

  Where the Ground Meets the Sky. Cavendish, 2002, ISBN 10761451058

Marguerite W. Davol

124 College Street, #19
South Hadley, MA 01075-7508
(413) 536-0422
davol@ttlc.net
<www.author-illustr-source.com/marguerite-davol.htm>
<www.authorsillustrators.com/davol/davol.htm>

 Award-winning author and storyteller Marguerite Davol offers age-related programs that cover the source of ideas, the importance of words, the writing process, and how stories become books. In addition, she talks about her own books and tells an original story. Communicating her own love of storytelling and books, Marguerite encourages children to enjoy creative thinking, pursue their desire to enjoy writing, and love books.

- Grade levels: K-6
- $$

- *Why Butterflies Go by on Silent Wings.* Illustrated by Rob Roth, Scholastic/Orchard, 2001, ISBN 0531303225, *Kirkus* starred review, Dr. Toy's Best 100 Children's Products, Dr. Toy's Ten Best Socially Responsible Products

  The Loudest, Fastest Best Drummer in Kansas. Illustrated by Cat Bowman Smith, Scholastic/Orchard, 2000, ISBN 0531301915

  The Paper Dragon. Illustrated by Robert Sabuda, Atheneum, 1997, ISBN 0689319924, American Booksellers Association Pick of the Lists, American Library Association Notable Book, National Council for Social Studies/Children's Book Council Notable, Parents' Choice Honor Book, Society of Children's Book Writers and Illustrators Golden Kite Award for text and illustrations

Norah Dooley

358 Washington Street
Cambridge, MA 02139
(617) 876-2422
(617) 497-6831 fax
Doochild6@aol.com

 With candor and wry humor, Norah Dooley tells the tale of how *Everybody Cooks Rice* finally made it into print, with the help of serendipity, hard work, and luck. She also shares life stories and folktales from her multicultural neighborhood to inspire beginning writers.

- Grade levels: K-12
- $$

- *Everybody Serves Soup.* Carolrhoda, 2000, ISBN 0876144121, Society of School Librarians International Social Studies Honor Book 2001

  Everybody Cooks Rice. Carolrhoda, 1991, ISBN 0876144121

  Everybody Bakes Bread. Carolrhoda, 1991, ISBN 0876144121, American Library Association Pick of the Lists

- Requirements: Microphone, table, slide projector, TV/VCR

Norman H. Finkelstein

56 Greenleaf Circle
Framingham, MA 01701
(508) 875-6419
biowriter@hotmail.com
<www.normfinkelstein.com>

Norman Finkelstein is the author of 12 historical biography books for young readers, and he enjoys speaking to students about the writing and publishing process. Norman loves to tell fascinating true stories that sometimes sound like fiction—a tribute to his storytelling power. He's won the National Jewish Book Award, the Golden Kite Honor Award, and the Holzman Award.

- Grade levels: 6-12
- $$

Michael Francis

2143 Commonwealth Avenue
Auburndale, MA 02466
(617) 965-5653
(603) 698-6361 fax
mfrancis@mike-francis.com

Mike Francis portrays *Galileo and the Stargazer's Apprentice* by using more than 20 years of professional acting experience on stage, in film, and in television, as well as time served as a physical science and physics teacher. He was also a lecturer at the Hayden Planetarium at the Boston Museum of Science.

- Grade levels: K-12
- $

Jack Gantos

45 Concord Square #1
Boston, MA 02118
(617) 267-5405
(617) 267-5406 fax
jgantos@mindspring.com (teachers only, please)

 Jack Gantos, author of more than 30 books ranging from primary readers to novels, tailors his creative writing and literature presentations to the audience.

- Grade levels: K-8
- $$$$
- *Rotten Ralph Helps Out.* Farrar, Straus & Giroux, 2001, ISBN 0374363552. The *Rotten Ralph* series is listed as an American Library Association Best Books for Beginning Readers

  Jack on the Tracks. Farrar, Straus & Giroux, 2000, ISBN 0374336652. The *Jack Henry* series has been listed on 100 Best Books by the New York Public Library

  Joey Pigza Loses Control. Farrar, Straus & Giroux, 2000, ISBN 0374399891, Newbery Honor Book
- Requirements: Carousel slide projector, overhead projector, large screen, microphone

Nancy Garden

c/o McIntosh and Otis
353 Lexington Avenue
New York, NY 10016
nancegar@aol.com
<www.nancygarden.com>

Where do you get ideas? Why do you write a particular book? How do you become a writer? How much money do writers make? What do you do when you get stuck? Nancy Garden never tires of answering these familiar questions when she talks with kids. She uses props and creative dramatics to help kids invent stories and she shares book contracts, messy revised manuscripts, and true stories about the writing process. She's been awarded the Robert B. Downs Intellectual Freedom Award.

- Grade levels: 4-12
- $$
- *Holly's Secret.* Farrar, Straus & Giroux, 2000, ISBN 0374332738, Lambda Book Award finalist, New York Public Library book for the Teen Age

  The Year They Burned the Books. Farrar, Straus & Giroux, 1999, ISBN 0374386676, Lambda Book Award finalist

  Dove & Sword: A Novel of Joan of Arc. Farrar, Straus & Giroux, 1995, ISBN 0374344760, New York Public Library Book for the Teen Age

Michael Glaser

PO Box 113
Fiskdale, MA 01518
(508) 347-2039
(561) 619-3361 fax
michaeljg@charter.net
<www.curiositycrew.com/michaelglaser>

 Live ocean animals are a highlight of the unusual program given by author, illustrator, and marine educator Michael Glaser. He shows kids the original artwork and rough drafts from his popular seashore books and explains to them that he has to work at his writing as hard as they work at theirs. His workshops give students an opportunity to see and touch tide-pool animals and to create a story about one of them. Michael's humorous, motivational, and informative workshops have reached more than 200,000 children in New England during the past 15 years.

- Grade levels: K-6
- $
- *Insect Investigations.* Knickerbocker Publishing, 1994, ISBN 0911635068

  The Nature of the Seashore. Knickerbocker Publishing, 1985, ISBN 0911635025

  Does Anyone Know Where a Hermit Crab Goes? Knickerbocker Publishing, 1983, ISBN 0911635009

Dara Goldman

430 Dutton Road
Sudbury, MA 01776
(978) 440-8636
(978) 440-9709 fax
Darasart@aol.com
<www.daragoldman.com>

Dara Goldman has been sketching animals and funny little figures since she was a child. Now, she's assembled an educational program to show children, step-by-step, what it takes to put together a children's book. She takes her audience "backstage" in her studio and shares a funny drawing game as her finale.

- Grade levels: K-8
- $$

Who Is Sam Harrington? Zondervan, 2000, ISBN 0310232031

Let's Play Hide and Seek. Scholastic, 1997, ISBN 0590929607

Merry Christmas Pop-up. Andrews McMeel, 1997, ISBN 0836236424

Beatrice Gormley

bgormley@bestweb.net
<www.webcom.com/bgormley>

Beatrice Gormley tells the story of how she became a writer during a presentation that helps students identify with the struggle to achieve a dream. In kids' excitement about writing and reading, they share their own struggles with and joy in writing. Beatrice also shares ideas on how to write well.

- Grade levels: 3-6
- $$
- *Laura Ingalls Wilder, Young Pioneer* (*Childhood of Famous Americans* series). Simon & Schuster/Aladdin, 2001, ISBN 0689839243

  President George W. Bush, Our 43rd President. Simon & Schuster/Aladdin, 2000, ISBN 068984123x

  Back to the Titanic (*Travelers Through Time* series). Scholastic, 1994, ISBN 0590462261
- Requirements: Table

Bonnie Greenburg

63 Gould Road
Newton, MA 02468
(617) 244-2884
BBonnieG@aol.com
<www.BonnieGreenberg.net>

Bonnie Greenberg uses storytelling as a teaching tool and tells engaging, vibrant stories rooted in her Appalachian childhood, her experiences in Israel, and tales from around the globe. Using guitar and song, she touches kids' hearts and minds with compelling tales from Japan, Ghana, Mexico, and the Middle East, including Holocaust Remembrance and Jewish folklore.

- Grade levels: K-12
- $$
- *From the Hearts of the People.* Hargreen Studios, 1996, ISBN 096601609 cassette, Parents' Choice Award, *Storytelling World* Winner's Award

  The Wonder Child and Other Young Heroes. Hargreen Studios, 2000, ISBN 0966016017 CD, National Association of Parenting Publications Association Gold Award, *Storytelling World* Award, Oppenheim Toy Award
- Requirements: Lapel microphone

Judith Jango-Cohen

23 Sarah Street
Burlington, MA 01803
(781) 229-6317 phone/fax
janelco@gis.net
<www.agpix.com/cohen>

From Scrap Paper to End Paper is Judith Jango-Cohen's behind-the-scenes look at the making of a book, in which she shares with students her works' scrap-paper beginnings, editor's suggestions, fact checker's comments, and layouts, as well as book reviews and letters from readers.

- Grade levels: K-12
- $$
- *Animals Animals* series. Marshall Cavendish, 2002, various ISBNs

  Pull Ahead series. Lerner, 2001, various ISBNs

  Animal Ways series. Marshall Cavendish, 2001, various ISBNs

Norton Juster

259 Lincoln Avenue
Amherst, MA 01002
(413) 549-6883
(413) 549-8506 fax

Norton Juster talks about the process of writing, fantasy and imagination, ideas and where they come from, the development of stories, and what being a writer means. He reads from his books and short-film scripts, discussing how a story is adapted from one medium to another. What he likes best, though, is responding to questions from students.

- Grade levels: 4-8

- $$$

- *As Silly as Knees, as Busy as Bees.* Beechtree, 1998, ISBN 0688163602

  Otter Nonsense. Morrow, 1994, ISBN 0688122833

  The Phantom Tollbooth. Random House, 1988 (reissue), ISBN 0394815009

- Requirements: TV/VCR

Jackie French Koller

jackiek@aol.com
<www.jackiefrenchkoller.com>

Jackie Koller's typical presentation involves a slide show and discussion of how she became a writer, where her ideas come from, and the writing process (and rejection—lots of it), as well as a glimpse into her scintillating and glamorous life as a writer.

- Grade levels: K-12

- $$

- *Someday.* Orchard, 2002, ISBN 0439293170

  Baby for Sale. Cavendish, 2002, ISBN 0761451064

  Mole and Shrew Find a Clue. Random House, 2001, ISBN 037580692X

- Requirements: Carousel slide projector, microphone

Stephen Krensky

Lexington, MA
c/o Simon & Schuster Library Marketing Author Appearance Hotline
(212) 698-2300

Stephen Krensky discusses his experiences with the writing and rewriting processes, and plays word games with students. He focuses on one or two of his ideas, discusses how they become stories, then reads the story aloud to show kids the end result.

- Grade levels: K-6

- $$$

- *We Just Moved.* Scholastic, 1998, ISBN 0590331272

  Children of the Earth and Sky. Scholastic, 1992, ISBN 0590428535, 0590468618 (Spanish)

  Fraidy Cats. Scholastic, 1993, ISBN 0590464388

Don Lessem

21 Bemuth Road
Newton, MA 02461
(617) 527-7796
(617) 527-7752 fax
Dinodonl@aol.com
<www.dinosaurdon.com>

The world's leading interpreter of dinosaurs; author of 25 dinosaur books; and advisor for *Jurassic Park,* Disney movies, and theme parks, "Dino Don" Lessem brings dinosaurs to your school for an exciting presentation of real and rare fossils, video, and lots of kid participation. He deals with reality vs. movie fantasy, history of life on earth, and a dinosaur's place in time, as well as the dinosaur's unique anatomy and, of course, what killed these animals.

- Grade levels: K-6

- $-$$$

- *Baby Dinosaurs.* Grosset & Dunlap, 2001, ISBN 044042536x

  Dinosaurs to Dodos. Scholastic, 1999, ISBN 0590316842

  Dinosaur Worlds. Boyds Mills, 1996, ISBN 1563975971

- Requirements: TV/VCR, table for skull of large meat-eater (optional for cost of shipping)

Rona Leventhal

PO Box 495
Hadley, MA 01035
(413) 586-0624
(413) 586-6655 fax
ronatales@mindspring.com

Rona Leventhal, a storyteller and movement and drama specialist, teaches students how skies talk, turtles sing, and magic happens as she weaves tales from many cultures to create a joyful sense of community.

- Grade levels: K-12
- $$
- *Spinning Tales, Weaving Hope: Stories of Peace, Justice and the Environment.* New Society of Publishers, 2002, ISBN 0865714479

Brian Lies

108 King Phillips Path
Duxbury, MA 02332
(781) 319-0456 phone/fax
<www.brianlies.com>

Brian Lies takes students on an entertaining journey into the world of making children's books, from developing ideas to early sloppy copies of text and pictures, through labor-intensive revisions, and finally, to a finished book. Aspiring authors and illustrators see original artwork, including Brian's own elementary school drawings and current works; hear stories about working as an author and illustrator; and see a live drawing demonstration, as Brian creates a new animal character with audience assistance.

- Grade levels: K-8
- $$
- *Hamlet and the Magnificent Sandcastle.* Moon Mountain Publishing, 2001, ISBN 0967792924

  See the Yak Yak. By Charles Ghigna, Random House, 1999, ISBN 0679891358

  Flatfoot Fox and the Case of the Missing Eye. By Eth Clifford, Houghton Mifflin, 1990, ISBN 0395519454

- Requirements: Easel, chair, table

Barbara Lipke

799 Commonwealth Avenue
Newton Centre, MA 02549
(617) 244-5606
bliptales@earthlink.net

Barbara Lipke's stories touch the heart, bring smiles of recognition, and often have audiences on the edges of their seats. In addition to telling stories for all ages, she presents workshops nationally for teachers and is involved in many organizations that foster the art of storytelling.

- Grade levels: K-12
- $
- *Figures, Facts and Fables: Telling Tales in Science and Math.* Heinemann, 1996, ISBN 043507105x

Tom McCabe

PO Box 128
Northampton, MA 01060
(413) 586-3353
ShoesNews@aol.com
<www.TomMcCabe.com>

Tom McCabe is New England's Pied Piper. He's toured the U.S. and abroad sharing original and traditional stories with more than a million people as a "teaching teller." Tom also leads students in writing programs that help them create original stories. He's a Parents' Choice Award winner and a Kennedy Center Millennium Artist.

- Grade levels: K-12
- $$
- *Stories Just for You.* Cassette, self-published, no date, no ISBN, Parents' Choice Award

  TNT (Tom's New Tape). Self-published, no date, no ISBN

  The Queen of Filene's Basement. Self-published, no date, no ISBN

Judith Moffatt

13 Charles Street
Medway, MA 02053-1613
(508) 533-4496
(508) 533-4574 fax
hoffmoff@judithmoffatt.com
<www.judithmoffatt.com>

Judith Moffatt, a cut-paper illustrator and author with more than 40 books to her credit, unlocks the mystery of how a two-dimensional drawing becomes a three-dimensional, cut-paper illustration during her one-hour presentation, which includes a slide show. Students see the step-by-step process of how her cut-paper art is constructed, photographed, and sent to a publisher, then Judith shares her technical secrets with the kids.

- Grade levels: K-4
- $$
- *Bugs.* Scholastic, 2001, ISBN 04390985899

  Too Many Rabbits. Scholastic, 2001, ISBN 0590967487

  Sunmaid Raisin Playbook. Simon & Schuster, 1999, ISBN 0689831307

- Requirements: Slide projector, art materials for each child (glue sticks, colored paper, scissors)

Barbara O'Connor

27 Simmons Drive
Duxbury, MA 02332
(781) 934-0166
(781) 934-3213 fax
barboc@aol.com

Barbara O'Connor discusses the process of writing a biography, including using factual material to write an interesting "story." She also offers a fiction program that covers how to turn a basic idea into a story, useful writing tools for effective writing, and how authors use real-life experiences to create fiction.

- Grade levels: 4-6
- $
- *Moonpie and Ivy.* Farrar, Straus & Giroux, 2001, ISBN 0374350590

Me and Rupert Goody. Farrar, Straus & Giroux, 1999, ISBN 0374349045

Beethoven in Paradise. Farrar, Straus & Giroux, 1997, ISBN 0374306664

Sydelle Pearl

75 Park Street, Apt. 1
Brookline, MA 02446
(617) 277-6488
pearldell@hotmail.com

Sydelle Pearl is a storyteller, an author, a songwriter, and a former children's librarian who incorporates into her presentations original songs that spring from the multicultural folktales she tells. She also leads sessions on incorporating songs and chants into storytimes, and offers imagination games and creative writing exercises.

- Grade levels: K-5
- $$
- *Elijah's Tears: Stories for the Jewish Holidays.* Henry Holt, 1996, ISBN 0805046275, American Booksellers Association Pick of the Lists, *Storytelling World* Award, Bank Street College Children's Book Committee Best Book 1998

Heidi Elisabet Yolen Stemple

Box 27
Hatfield, MA 01036
(413) 247-5016
HeidiEYS@aol.com

Heidi Stemple grew up around books—lots of books. Her mother, Jane Yolen, has authored more than 200 books, including the 1988 Caldecott Award winner *Owl Moon*, which is a story about Heidi and her father. Now a writer herself, Heidi visits schools to share tales of her childhood among (and even in) books. Students love her funny, eye-rolling, poetry readings and her discussion of how a book is created—a step-by-step process that's similar, Heidi points out, to what kids do in school every day.

- Grade levels: K-8
- $$

- *Dear Mother/Dear Daughter: Poems for Young People.* Boyds Mills, 2001, ISBN 1563978865

- *Unsolved Mysteries from History* series *(The Mary Celeste, The Wolf Girls, Lost Colony of Roanoke).* Simon & Schuster, 1999-2002, various ISBNs

- *Meet the Monsters.* Walker, 1996, ISBN 0802784410

- Requirements: Library venue

Jane Sutton

11 Mason Street
Lexington, MA 02421
(781) 862-5186
jsutton65@rcn.com

Jane Sutton's program takes kids from the moment of first inspiration to opening fan letters. She talks about the trials and rewards of being an author and shows students overheads of messy drafts, clean-typed manuscripts, rejection slips, and galleys. She also emphasizes the importance of rewriting *a lot.*

- Grade levels: 3-5

- $

- *The Trouble with Cauliflower.* Dial, 2003, ISBN 0803727070

- Requirements: Overhead slide projector

Tony Toledo

PO Box 302
Beverly, MA 01915
(978) 921-4628
(978) 927-9749 fax
ToledoGoat@aol.com
<www.TonyToledo.com>

If you need to lubricate your brain-to-ear connection, Tony Toledo's tales are right for you. From *The Scary Hand* to *Summer on Two Wheels*, Tony will have you laughing one minute and misty-eyed the next. He says he's 43 years old but reads at a 55-year-old level and would like to come to your school to fill your ears.

- Grade levels: K-6 (but he'll tell ghost stories to middle schoolers)

- $-$$

- *Ten Tales by Tony Toledo.* CoveArts.com, 1996, cassette, self-published, no ISBN

Joy Nelkin Wieder

25 Oneida Road
Acton, MA 01720
(978) 263-1686
(978) 266-9320 fax
jnweider@attbi.com

Joy Wieder offers lively, interactive programs that highlight historical fiction, illustration, and family genealogy, and a presentation on Jewish books that details three significant areas: the Sabbath, family, and ancient Israel.

- Grade levels: 2-6

- $

- *At the End of the Tunnel.* Hachai Publishing, forthcoming

- *The Great Potato Plan.* Hachai Publishing, 1999, ISBN 0780922613892

- *Let's Talk about the Sabbath.* By Dorothy K. Kripke, co-illustrated with Stacy Crossland, Alef Design Group, 1999, ISBN 0781881283188

- Requirements: Overhead projector, easel

Jane Yolen

PO Box 27
Hatfield, MA 01038
(413) 247-5016
(413) 247-9659 fax
janeyolen@aol.com
<www.janeyolen.com>

Jane Yolen is the author of more than 200 books, some of which have won the Caldecott, the Christopher, the Nebula, the Jewish Book Award, or the Mythopoetic Society Award, as well as state, storytelling, and science fiction awards. She also has six body-of-work awards and two honorary doctorates. She no longer does school visits, but enjoys young author conferences, storytelling events, and major writing conferences.

- $$$$

Michigan

Betty Appleton

1511 East Maple Road
Birmingham, MI 48009
(248) 644-5496
appleton@Oakland.edu

Betty Appleton turns a simple story into an exciting opportunity for her listeners to sing, move, and explore rhythms. Her extensive experience teaching dance, music, and rhythm, and her large collection of percussion instruments well equip her to offer an exciting, multidimensional approach to storytelling.

- Grade levels: K-5, adults
- $
- "Making Alphabet Shapes." In *Leap, Skip Twist and Freeze,* edited by Kate O'Neill, Michigan Dance Assn., 1979, no ISBN
- Requirements: Two tables, two chairs

Tim Bogar

2513 Woodruff
Lansing, MI 48912
(517) 372-4141
timbogar@voyager.net

Storyteller Tim Bogar writes his own material, including animal stories, adventures, romances, and healing tales.

- Grade levels: K-12
- $

Jean S. Bolley

12147 Chandler Road
Bath, MI 48808
(517) 886-0843
bolleyj@hotmail.com

Jean Bolley specializes in world folktales and Michigan history, and uses puppets, string stories, audience participation, and paper folding in her programs. She also gives workshops for teachers and offers bibliographies of related materials.

- Grade levels: K-12
- $
- Requirements: Sound equipment

Linda Dick

5385 Swallow Avenue
Kalamazoo, MI 49009
(616) 375-8520
(616) 353-3560 fax
linda-dick@att.net

Are You a Wannabe Writer? Me Too! is Linda Dick's presentation introducing students to the writing life. She helps young writers find a subject they're comfortable writing about and expand their confidence and writing abilities. She encourages them to write from the heart, to use current events as a starting point, and to learn all forms of writing, from poetry and short story to novel, drama, and screenplay.

- Grade levels: 3-12
- $

Christopher Jay Dodge

164 Carriage Way
Ypsilanti, MI 48197
(734) 434-0331 phone/fax
dodgej@saline.k12.mi.us

■ *The Greatest Show on Earth* is what Chris Dodge calls his presentation on being an illustrator. He tells kids stories of how he got started and about the art classes he survived, and gives them practical information such as the proper way to prepare a portfolio for presentation. He demonstrates the steps of designing and completing a book cover, then completes the presentation with a drawing that kids can draw along with.

■ Grade levels: K-12

■ $

■ *The Puffin Pilfer.* Jou-Jou Productions, 1999, ISBN 1929290012

The Plover Lover. Jou-Jou Productions, 1999, ISBN 1929290004

■ Requirements: Slide projector, two tables, sound system

Diane Youngblood Donlon

4335 Lake Michigan Drive NW, Suite 127
Grand Rapids, MI 49544
(616) 735-0553
(616) 791-8005 fax
Diane921@hotmail.com
<www.ollypublishing.com>

■ "Miss Diane" is a wiggle-worm expert whose presentations integrate story acting, music, and movement to encourage children to become storytellers, dancers, and singers.

■ Grade levels: K-3

■ $$

■ Requirements: CD player, microphone, slide projector

Sid "The Rock" Ellis

1416 Egleston
Kalamazoo, MI 49001
(616) 344-2418
sidtherock@msn.com

■ Sid "The Rock" Ellis presents puppetry and storytelling in a participatory program of "edutainment" that includes humor, education, and whimsical wholesomeness. He's been producing, writing, and performing puppetry for many years.

■ Grade levels: K-12

■ $

■ Requirements: Sound system, CD player

Jean Alicia Elster

1010 Stafford Place
Detroit, MI 48207
(313) 392-9355
(313) 566-0052 fax
elsterusa@mac.com

■ Jean Elster draws her listeners into stories by interspersing her reading with tidbits about character development and the real events that were used to create a fictional tale.

■ Grade levels: 1-5

■ $

■ *I Have a Dream, Too!* Judson Press, 2002, ISBN 0817013970

Just Call Me Joe Joe. Judson Press, 2001, ISBN 0817013989

Rhonda Gowler Greene

5459 Claridge
West Bloomfield, MI 48322
(248) 851-1518
rgowgreene@hotmail.com
<www.rhondagowlergreene.com>

■ Rhonda Greene offers slide presentations that give an inside view of how books are made, from idea to bound copy, and shows rejections, galleys, page proofs, and huge print sheets. She sometimes combines this method with the use of puppets, African instruments, and spirited readings of books.

■ Grade levels: K-8

- $$$
- *Eek! Creak! Snicker, Sneak.* Simon & Schuster, 2002, ISBN 06898304705

  Barnyard Song. Simon & Schuster, 1997, ISBN 0689807588, 0689840543 pbk

  When a Line Bends... a Shape Begins. Houghton Mifflin, 1997, ISBN 0395786061, 0618152415 pbk
- Requirements: Slide projector, screen, microphone

Sandra Hansen

227 West 19th Street
Holland, MI 49423
(616) 396-5772 or (800) 484-1773 code 7638
(616) 396-4023 fax (call first)
shansen@wmol.com
<www.wmol.com/whalive>

In her performance, *Women's History Alive!*, Sandra Hansen portrays famous women from the American past. Sandra's written and performed five one-woman plays, including *Kate's Pants* (famous women), *Civil War Women* (five women's diaries), *Miss Fuller's Letter* (dreaming of college), *Chewing Gum Junk Shop* (20th-century women), and *Michigan Magic* (teaching women's history using magic tricks).

- Grade levels: K-12
- $$

Yvonne Healy

5193 King Road
Howell, MI 48843
(800) 760-9233 ext. 29
(810) 225-2204
healy@cac.net
<www.yHealy.com>

A born storyteller, Yvonne Healy was raised in the Irish oral tradition before growing up to act in New York theaters and comedy clubs. Children led her heart back to storytelling, however, where she uses voice, gesture, and story to invite audiences into the theater of their imagination. Yvonne uses myths, folktales, and history to tickle kids' funny bones and touch their hearts, while stretching their imaginations and raising their spirits. Her stories cover a wide range of sources, including Celtic, European, Asian, Pacific, and Hispanic traditions.

- Grade levels: K-12
- $
- Requirements: Sound system

Kevin Kammeraad

3148 Plainfield NE, PMB 248
Grand Rapids, MI 49525
(877) 986-6286
(616) 364-5871 fax
Kevin@tomatocollection.com
<www.tomatocollection.com>

Kevin Kammeraad visits schools to have fun with kids through creative writing, music, art, and puppetry. He encourages his audience to explore the arts by sharing the process of how he created his book and CD. He uses visual aids and involves students, and everyone has a good time.

- Grade levels: K-5
- $$
- *The Tomato Collection.* Cooperfly Books, 1999, ISBN 096695042

  The Tomato Collection, CD, 1999, ISBN 0966950410

Linda Luke

47762 Northshore Drive
Belleville, MI 48111
(732) 697-9275
lukeatlake@aol.com

Linda Luke has enhanced her 30-year career as an elementary teacher by telling stories at schools, festivals, camps, hospitals, bookstores, funeral homes, and Christmas events. She's taught all ages how to tell a good story—and shown them how by doing it herself.

- Grade levels: K-6
- $$
- Requirements: Cordless microphone

Shirley Neitzel

5060 Sequoia SE
Grand Rapids, MI 49512
(616) 698-8849
seneitzel@aol.com

Using costumes and props, Shirley Neitzel treats children to an adventure in rhyme and rebus as she has them help act out dramatic readings from her picture books. She offers older students a glimpse of Native American culture by reading Ojibwa legends and shares her writing process, from idea to finished book.

- Grade levels: K-6
- $
- *I'm Taking a Trip on My Train.* With Nancy Winslow Parker, Greenwillow, 1999, ISBN 0688158331

  The Bag I'm Taking to Grandma's. With Nancy Winslow Parker, Mulberry, 1998, ISBN 0688158404

  We're Making Breakfast for Mother. Greenwillow, 1997, ISBN 0688145752

- Requirements: Slide projector, large space for children to move in

Ann Gieseler Bryan Nelson

502 Linden Avenue
Albion, MI 49224
(517) 629-4069
agbnelson@hotmail.com

Mother Goose rides again on Annie Nelson's "goose stick," which inspires young children to participate in group chants of these ancient rhymes. She also tells tales of the Norwegian trolls who came to destroy Christmas, as well as stories from various other cultures. She includes booktalks in many of her sessions and involves children in choral reading to encourage more engagement with books.

- Grade levels: K-6
- $
- Requirements: Sound system

Barbara G. Schutzgruber

2855 Kimberly
Ann Arbor, MI 48104-6454
(734) 761-5118
Barbara@BGS-Story.com
<www.BGS-Story.com>

Enhanced by her rich voice and flawless pacing, Barbara Schutzgruber's lively and spontaneous style combines words, string, and song to weave images and hold her audiences spellbound with trickster tales, ghost stories, string stories, world folktales, medieval epics and ballads, and stories of gutsy girls and wise women.

- Grade levels: K-12
- $$
- *String Things: Stories, Games and More.* Video, self-published, no date, no ISBN

  Still a Bit of Sugar but even More Spice: More Stories of Gutsy Girls and Wise Women. CD, self-published, no date, no ISBN

  Ladies' Night Out. CD, self-published, no date, no ISBN

Lois Sprengnether

5640 Farley Road
Clarkston, MI 48046
(248) 625-5848
LoiSsez@earthlink.net

Lois Sprengnether tells stories from the Great Lakes, as well as from Australia, Africa, and other continents. She also offers spooky stories, Native American tales (especially Anishinabe Chippewa), tall tales, and Paul Bunyan tales, all with and without puppet and sign language. Lois is a certified Word Weaving instructor who's been telling stories since 1970.

- Grade levels: K-6
- $$

Corinne Stavish

26216 Franklin Pointe Drive
Southfield, MI 48034
(248) 356-8721
(248) 204-3518 fax
Stavish@LTU.edu
<www.storynet.org>

A freelance teller for almost 20 years, Corinne Stavish specializes in school programs that focus on problem-solving, justice, and comparative world folklore. She offers Hasidic stories, fairy tales, women's stories (including biblical), and Cinderella-across-cultures stories. She also teaches storytelling and offers lectures on related topics.

- Grade levels: K-12

- $-$$

- *Seeds from Our Past: Planting for the Future.* B'nai B'rith Center for Jewish Identity, 1996, ISBN 0910240316

  Tales Through the Ages for All Ages. Cassette, self-published, no date, no ISBN

  Women: Willful, Witty Wise. Cassette, self-published, no date, no ISBN

Allison Stoutland

PO Box 15
Okemos, MI 48805
(517) 349-9770 phone/fax
astoutland@aol.com
<www.inchbyinchbooks.com>

Allison Stoutland's multifaceted program includes readings from her books and telling the story behind the story about the process of writing, illustrating, and publishing books.

- Grade levels: K-12

- $

- *Put Your Best Foot Forward: More Lessons for a Happier World.* Inch by Inch, 2000, ISBN 0967094119

  Reach for the Sky and Other Little Lessons for a Happier World. Inch by Inch, 1999, ISBN 0967094100

Mississippi

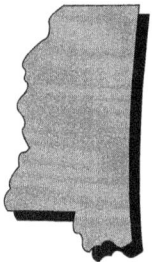

Sylvia B. Williams

Route 1, Box 301
West Point, MS 39773
(662) 494-3547
windyhill_wp@yahoo.com
<www.southernbreeze.org>

Sylvia Williams, who's an elementary teacher and librarian as well as a writer, encourages students to be readers by sharing her 30 years of experience working with books and children, and offering insights into the writing process. She also urges youngsters to apply her techniques to their own writing.

- Grade levels: K-8

- $

- *Paul "Bear" Bryant: Football Legend.* Seacoast Publishing, 2002, ISBN 1878561928

   Alex Haley, I Have a Dream. Abdo Publishing, 1996, ISBN 156239570x

   "The Singing River." In *Stories from Where We Live* (Gulf Coast volume), Milkweed, 2002, ISBN 1571316361

- Requirements: Dry-erase board, markers

New Hampshire

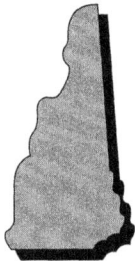

Mary Emma Allen

55 Binks Hill Road
Plymouth, NH 03264
(603) 536-4851 fax
Me.allen@juno.com
<homepage.fcgnetworks.net/jetent/mea>

Author and illustrator Mary Emma Allen's programs encourag young writers by teaching them to have fun with poetry, to create imaginary characters, to discover story ideas, and to make history come alive. She also teaches kids about writing on the Internet, illustrating your stories, and the life of a reporter. One of her favorite presentations is on quilt history and is based on her book of quilt projects for kids.

- Grade levels: K-12
- $
- *Writing in Maine, New Hampshire and Vermont.* Writers World Press, 1997, ISBN 0963144154

  Tales of Adventure and Discovery. MEA Productions, 1996, ISBN 096516750x
- Requirements: Whiteboard with markers, sound system, overhead projector

Odds Bodkin

PO Box 410
Bradford, NH 03221
(603) 938-5120
(603) 938-5616 fax
rivertree@mcttelecom.com
<www.oddsbodkin.com>

Odds Bodkin travels far and wide sharing his stories with eager listeners. He accompanies his tales with original music on guitars, Celtic harp, piano, and pipes, and uses more than 100 character voices and vocal effects. He's won Parents' Choice Silver and Gold awards, *Storytelling World* awards, and many others.

- Grade levels: K-12
- $$$
- *Adventures of Little Proto.* Rivertree Productions, 2001, ISBN 1882412133 cassette

  Christmas Cobwebs. Harcourt Brace, 2001, ISBN 0152014594

  The Rage of Hercules. Rivertree Productions, 2000, ISBN 188241232x CD, 1882412311 cassette
- Requirements: Stage, sturdy armless chair, two boom microphones

Chris Demarest

PO Box 1280
Lebanon, NH 03766
(603) 442-9567
Chris.L.Demarest@Valley.net

Chris Demarest knows that art is about making mistakes, so his presentation begins with a squiggle that turns into a story—but during this process, a "mistake" gets made that makes the drawing better. Chris also shows students how to make simple pop-ups and shares slides of his current work and research.

- Grade levels: K-12

- $$
- *Smokejumpers One to Ten.* Simon & Schuster/McElderry, 2002, ISBN 0689841205
- *The Cowboy ABC.* DK Publishing, 2001, ISBN 0789481901
- *Firefighters A to Z.* Simon & Schuster/McElderry, 2000, ISBN 0689837984
- Requirements: Slide projector, TV/VCR, easel, large newsprint pad, markers

Ralph Fletcher

PO Box 855
Durham, NH 03824
(603) 659-0628
fletcher17@earthlink.net
<www.ralphfletcher.com>

Take a peek into Ralph Fletcher's writing notebook, where he collects "seed ideas" that often flower into books. Ralph shares stories from his books and tells tales about being a writer across genres—chapter books, poetry, picture books, and series books.

- Grade levels: K-12
- $$$
- *Twilight Comes Twice.* Clarion, 1997, ISBN 0395848261
- *A Writer's Notebook.* HarperCollins, 1996, ISBN 0380784300
- *Fig Pudding.* Clarion, 1996, ISBN 044041203x

Ross Kenyon

27 Gilmore Pond Road
Jaffrey, NH 03452
(603) 532-4113
rosskenyon@msn.com

A captivating storyteller and award-winning entertainer, Ross Kenyon offers a wealth of folktales, legends, Native American stories, local stories, classic tales, and stories for the spirit and heart. When Ross tells a story, be it a tall tale, myth, or legend, one thing is certain—his audiences are carried away on a whirlwind of adventure, introduced to a new age, and perhaps even taught a lesson. Ross also encourages audience participation.

- Grade levels: K-12
- $
- Requirements: None—brings own sound system

Angela Cay Klingler

PO Box 530
Salem, NH 03079
(603) 898-0537
AKFairTale@aol.com
<members.aol.com/AKFairTale>

Angela Klingler's creative, animated tellings and retellings of traditional world folktales, fables, and fairy tales delight and engage the imaginations of all ages. Her programs promote a quest for knowledge, critical thinking, imagination, and character, and are filled with awe and wonder. In her *Faire Tales* presentation she dresses as The Storyteller who travels with a huge, quilted tapestry banner and story stick, as in the days of yore.

- Grade levels: K-12
- $
- *Faire Tales.* Cassette, self-published, no date, ISBN 0965023214

Brownie Macintosh and Julie Thompson

Grebrd@aol.com
brownie@juliebrownie.com
<www.juliebrownie.com>

Julie Thompson and Brownie Macintosh's show combines original and traditional music, sign language, and a serious specialty—pirates!

- Grade levels: K-12
- $
- *A Pirate's Life for Me.* Charlesbridge, 1996, ISBN 0881068357

Ryan Thomson

4 Elm Court
Newmarket, NH 03857
(6030 659-2658
cfiddle@tiac.net
<www.captainfiddle.com>

Welcome to the world of Captain Fiddle, where Ryan Thomson demonstrates and plays folk instruments such as the fiddle, the banjo, the accordian, the flute, and the pennywhistle. He also shares examples of the books he's written, including their rough drafts, artwork, and final forms. Brian is the Northeast Regional winner of the National Fiddle Contest.

- Grade levels: K-12

- $

- *Banjo Tab Book.* Captain Fiddle Publications, 1999, ISBN 0931877296

  Fiddle and Violin Buyer's Guide. Captain Fiddle Publications, 1996, ISBN 0931877105

  Folk Musician's Working Guide to Chords, Keys, Scales and More. Captain Fiddle Publications, 1995, ISBN 0931877202

New Jersey

Danny and Kim Adlerman
(pen name: Kin Eagle)

47 Stoneham Place
Metuchen, NJ 08840
(732) 548-1779
(732) 548-4180 fax
bookkids@aol.com
<www.dannyandkim.com>

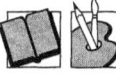 Children's author-musician-illustrator team Danny and Kim Adlerman, collaboratively known as Kin Eagle, bring a sense of fun and rhythm into the classrooms they visit by using original children's music, guitar, and voices. Kim sketches for the kids and shows them the illustration process, from sketch to dummy to final copy. Most of the duo's books have a musical element or basis.

■ Grade levels: K-6

■ $$

■ *Songs for America's Children.* The Kids at Our House Publishing, 2002, forthcoming

Africa Calling. Charlesbridge, 1996, ISBN 1879085984, 1580890253 pbk

It's Raining, It's Pouring. Charlesbridge, 1994, ISBN 1879085887, 1879088712 pbk

Pat Brisson

94 Bullman Street
Phillipsburg, NJ 08865
(908) 454-9455
brisson@enter.net
<www.enter.net/~brisson>

■ Pat Brisson's program, *Journey of a Picture Book from Idea to Finished Product*, features a slide presentation designed to show students that books are written by ordinary people (and therefore might be something students would do some day) and how a picture book goes from being an idea in someone's head to a finished product that you can hold in your hands and read.

■ Grade levels: K-5

■ $$$

■ *The Summer My Father Was Ten.* Boyds Mills, 1998, ISBN 1563974355, 1569378296 pbk, Christopher Award, Hodge Podger Award, Paterson Prize for Children's Literature, American Booksellers Association Pick of the Lists, *Booklist* starred review, *Kirkus* pointer review, International Reading Association Teacher's Choice

Hot Fudge Hero. Henry Holt, 1997, ISBN 0805045511, Parents' Choice Honor Book, New York Public Library 100 Best Books for Reading and Sharing

Wanda's Roses. Boyds Mills, 1994, ISBN 1563971364, 156397925X pbk, American Booksellers Association Pick of the Lists, New York Charlotte Award, Virginia Library Association Young Readers' Choice Award

■ Requirements: AV cart, sound system, screen

Margery Cuyler

32 Edgehill Street
Princeton, NJ 08540
(609) 921-2289

One of Margery Cuyler's talks, *Road Map of the Imagination*, includes slides of the haunted house where she grew up (and got the idea for her book *The Battlefield Ghost*). She discusses with students the choices authors make, reads aloud, and explains the different stages of book development. She also offers talks on *Creative Connections Between Books and the Internet* and the *Dual Personality of Being Both an Editor and a Writer*.

- Grade levels: 1-3
- $$$
- *Stop Drop and Roll.* Simon & Schuster, 2001, ISBN 0689843550

  100th Day Worries. Simon & Schuster, 2000, ISBN 06898299795

  That's Good! That's Bad. Henry Holt, 1993, ISBN 0805029540

- Requirements: Slide projector

Michael Dooling

161 Wyoming Avenue
Audubon, NJ 08106
(856) 546-6507
mtdool@aol.com
<www.michaeldooling.com>

Michael Dooling has always been fascinated with the past. Now, as the illustrator of more than 50 novels and picture books, he loves sharing that penchant with youngsters. He gives presentations in colonial costume and shares the whole process of illustrating a picture book, including how to mix colors, draw using simple shapes, and incorporate emotion.

- Grade levels: 1-8
- $$$
- *The Great Horseless Carriage Race.* Holiday House, 2002, ISBN 0823416402

  The Amazing Life of Benjamin Franklin. By James Cross Giblin, Scholastic, 2000, ISBN 0590485342

  The Memory Coat. By Elvira Woodruff, Scholastic, 1999, ISBN 059077179

Dan Gutman

224 Euclid Avenue
Haddonfield, NJ 08033
(856) 354-9031
dangut@aol.com
<www.dangutman.com>

Reading, writing, and sports—those are the things that Dan Gutman likes. In his programs, he uses sports to get kids (especially reluctant readers) interested in books, writing, and reading. He shows students how a book is conceived, researched, written, and published, then speaks about rejections and never giving up on your dreams. His programs also include narrative, a slide show, a writing workshop, and interaction.

- Grade levels: 2-6
- $$$
- *Honus and Me.* HarperCollins, 1997, ISBN 0380973502

  The Million Dollar Shot. Hyperion, 1997, ISBN 0786803347

  The Kid Who Ran For President. Scholastic, 1996, ISBN 0590939874

- Requirements: Slide projector, screen, cart, microphone, table

Arlene Hirschfelder

170 Copley Avenue
Teaneck, NJ 07666
(201) 836-0973
(201) 836-2361 fax
Arlene0417@aol.com

After 32 years teaching Native American studies, writing 18 nonfiction books about the history and contemporary realities of native peoples, and conducting many workshops, Arlene Hirschfelder can handle just about any Native American subject. She offers school programs designed to encourage young people to write and publish online or offline. Using exercises based on her award-winning book *Rising Voices: The Writings of Young Native Americans,* she also takes young people on a journey through the "5 Rs" of writing: revelation, research, revisions, reviews, and royalties.

- Grade levels: 3-12
- $-$$$
- *Native Americans: A History in Pictures.* DK, 2000, ISBN 078945162X, New York Public Library Book for the Teen Age, translated into five languages
- *Photo Odyssey: Solomon Carvalho's Remarkable Western Adventure, 1853-4.* Clarion, 2000, ISBN 039589123x, Association of Jewish Libraries Notable, National Council for Social Studies/Children's Book Council Notable, New York Public Library Book for the Teen Age
- *Rising Voices: The Writings of Young Native Americans.* Scribner, 1992, ISBN 0804111677, *Boston Globe* Choices for 25 Best in Children's Nonfiction, International Reading Association Children's Choice, New York Public Library Book for the Teen Age
- Requirements: Slide projector, sound system

Jan and Phil Huling

938 Bloomfield Street
Hoboken, NJ 07030
(201) 795-9366
(201) 792-6869 fax
janhuling@yahoo.com

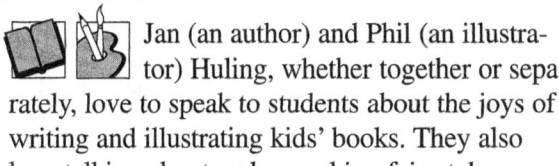 Jan (an author) and Phil (an illustrator) Huling, whether together or separately, love to speak to students about the joys of writing and illustrating kids' books. They also love talking about and reworking fairy tales.

- Grade levels: 3-6
- $
- *Puss in Cowboy Boots.* Simon & Schuster, 2002, ISBN 0689831196
- *Moses in Egypt.* Simon & Schuster, 1995, ISBN 0689802269
- Requirements: Easel, sound system if group is large

Laura Kaighn

Lady Hawke Storytelling
247 Hammond Drive
Williamstown, NJ 08094-1516
(856) 728-0816
laurakaighn@comcast.net

Laura Kaighn is known far and wide for her dynamic, expressive style and her use of realia, artifacts, and outfits to enhance her programs. Her topics include Celtic and dragon lore, nature stories and crafts, celestial tales, Greek and Egyptian mythology, scary stories, peace tales, and Native American stories (she's part Cherokee). She also conducts adult workshops: *Rabbit's Tail and Other Rites of Passage, Original Fables for a New Mythology,* and *Sharing Family Stories: Gifts from the Heart.*

- Grade levels: K-12
- $$

Susan Schott Karr

61 Woodland Road
Chatham, NJ 07929-2008
SusanKarr@aol.com
<www.wordsuite.com>

Susan Schott Karr presents *The Life and Times of Richard Feynman,* who was a Nobel Prize-winning physicist and one of the top 10 scientists of all time. Feynman's passion for the world of science, especially physics, was balanced by his adventures to strange exotic places; his love of drawing, painting, and playing the bongos; and his wonder-filled storytelling. Susan shares all of this with students during her presentation.

- Grade levels: 2-12
- $
- *Richard Feynman.* Viking, forthcoming
- Requirements: TV/VCR, CD/cassette player

Marylou Moran Kjelle

P.O. Box 4204
Metuchen, NJ 08840
(908) 756-9557
(908) 755-4473 fax
marmorano@aol.com
<www.mmoranokjelle.com>

Marylou Kjelle teaches students how to write a biography by showing them the outlining techniques she utilizes in her own books. Follow-up contact with students includes feedback from the author and helps them integrate what they've learned.

- Grade levels: 4-7
- $
- *The Waco Siege.* Chelsea House, 2002, ISBN 0791067394

  Helping Hands: A City and a Nation Lend Support at Ground Zero. Chelsea House, 2002, ISBN 0791069591

  Raymond Damadian and the Story of MRI. Mitchell Lane, 2002, ISBN 1584151412
- Requirements: Flip chart, place to tape up wall charts

Sandy Lanton

37 Juneau Boulevard
Woodbury, NJ 11797
(516) 367-3984
slanton@ivillage.com
<www.sandylanton.com>

Sandy Lanton shows younger students how a picture book is created and discusses the writing process. She gives older students writing exercises and discusses with them how to select good books and handle difficult subjects through picture books. Sandy also offers a workshop about explaining death to children.

- Grade levels: K-12
- $
- *Daddy's Chair.* Lanton Haas Press, 2001, ISBN 0970248202, 0970248210 pbk, Sydney Taylor Award

  The Happy Hackers. The Wright Group, 1996, ISBN 0780241436 pbk
- Requirements: Chalkboard or paper on easel, opaque projector, slide projector

Frané Lessac

846 Saddle River Road
Saddle Brook, NJ 07663
(210) 791-2091
(210) 791-2139 fax
Artbeat@ozemail.com.au
<www.artbeatpublishers.com>

 Illustrator-author Frané Lessac's multicultural children's books have been translated into several languages and reflect her optimism, humor, and touch for detail, which delight students of all ages and abilities. Her presentation focuses on the process of creating a book, includes discussion of her 30 rejections and her 20 published titles, and emphasizes her mission to instill in children a sense of pride and self-esteem about their unique heritages and their abilities to capture it in words and pictures. Her titles have won a plethora of accolades and awards.

- Grade levels: K-12
- $$
- *On the Same Day in March.* By Marilyn Singer, HarperCollins, 2000, ISBN 0060281871, National Council for Social Studies/Children's Book Council Notable Trade Book in Social Studies, Booklist Top Ten Science Books

  Wonderful Towers of Watts. By Patricia Zelver, Morrow/Tambourine, 1994, ISBN 0688126502, Reading Rainbow Feature Book, Children's Books of Distinction Awards

  My Little Island. HarperCollins, 1985, ISBN 0397321155, Reading Rainbow Feature book, St. Marteen Children's Book of the Year
- Requirements: Carpet-covered easels for Velcro, black- or whiteboard, tape player

E. B. Lewis

1425 Mays Landing Road
Folsom, NJ 08037
(215) 387-1960 (R. Watson, for booking)
rashida.Watson@verizon.net
eblewis@eticomm.net
<www.eblewis.com>

 The talent of E. B. Lewis is evident in his artwork but also extends to his ability to teach and motivate people of all ages. Through

art, humor, and example, E. B.'s presentations have delighted audiences of all ages all over the country and the world.

- Grade levels: K-12
- $$

Sue Macy

185 East Palisade Avenue, D 11-B
Englewood, NJ 07631
(201) 567-3620
(201) 568-2924
SueMacy1@aol.com
<www.suemacy.com>

Sue Macy has done extensive research on pioneering female athletes from the 1800s to today. her slide show, *Forgotten Heroes of Women's Sports History,* introduces students to the struggles and victories of these determined women. She also offers a presentation on *Sharpshooter Annie Oakley* and one on the *All-American Girls Professional Baseball League.*

- Grade levels: 4-9
- $$
- *Bull's Eye: A Photobiography of Annie Oakley.* National Geographic Society, 2001, ISBN 0792270088, *School Library Journal* Best Books 2001, American Library Association Notable Book, National Parenting Publications Gold Medal, Children's Book Council Notable Book

  Winning Ways: A Photohistory of American Women in Sports. Henry Holt, 1996, ISBN 0805041478, *SLJ* Best Book, ALA Best Books for Young Adults, ALA Notable Book, *Booklist* Editors Choice

  A Whole New Ball Game: The Story of the All-American Girls Professional Baseball League. Henry Holt, 1993, ISBN 0805019421, 014037423x pbk, *SLJ* Best Books 1993, ALA Best Books for Young Adults, CBC Notable Trade Book in Field of Social Studies

- Requirements: Carousel slide projector w/remote control

Robert Matero

294 Maitland Avenue
Teaneck, NJ 07666
(201) 833-4846
Bookwizard99@aol.com

Bob Matero's slide presentation and discussion take kids behind the scenes to show them how a writer lives and works. Live animals are available for all presentations and provide a lively springboard for discussions on research and the writing process.

- Grade levels: 1-6
- $$
- *Animals Asleep.* Millbrook, 2000, ISBN 0761316523

  Lizards. Kidsbooks, 1997, ISBN 1561564719

  The Birth of a Humpback Whale. Atheneum, 1996, ISBN 0689319312

- Requirements: Slide projector, water for animals

Joyce McDonald

104 Cemetery Road
Blairstown, NJ 07825
(908) 496-4478
jmcdonald@nac.net or
joycemcdonald.net@nac.net
<www.joycemcdonald.net>

Through her humorous and engaging slide presentation, Joyce McDonald shares the excitement and fun of being a professional writer. She reveals the creative influences, the struggles, and the real-life events that inspired her stories and offers suggestions on how students might develop their own creative writing.

- Grade levels: 5-8
- $$
- *Shades of Simon Gray.* Random House/Delacorte, 2001, ISBN 0385326599

  Shadow People. Random House/Delacorte, 2000, ISBN 0385326629, 0440228077 pbk, New York Public Library Books for the Teen Age

  Swallowing Stones. Random House/Delacorte, 1997, ISBN 0385323093, 0440226724 pbk,

American Library Association Top Ten Best for Young Adults, *Booklist* Best of the Best 100, New York Public Library Books for the Teen Age, many other awards

- Requirements: AV cart, carousel slide projector, microphone

Tamara Petrosino

39 Hornblower Avenue
Belleville, NJ 07109
(973) 751-0692
(973) 751-2966 fax
tamarapetrosino@hotmail.com

Tamara Petrosino's school visits include a reading and a craft, such as making rabbit puppets out of paper bags or making bunny ears. For older students, she demonstrates how to illustrate a children's book.

- Grade levels: K-12

- $

- *The Worst Haircut Ever!* Publishing Partners, 2002, ISBN pending

  Rocky, the Cat Who Barks. Dutton, 2002, ISBN 0525465448

  Rabbit Stew. Grosset & Dunlap, 1999, ISBN 0448414937

Wendy Pfeffer

3 Timberlane Drive
Pennington, NJ 08534
(609) 737-1569 phone/fax
TomWendyPf@aol.com
<www.author-illustr-source.com/wendypfeffer.htm>

Wendy Pfeffer visits schools and shares her real-life, entertaining, and informative tales to help children discover the joy of writing. She also explains to students how her books move from being a spark of an idea to being words in print.

- Grade levels: K-6

- $$

- *A Log's Life.* Simon & Schuster, 1997, ISBN 0689806361, Outstanding Science Trade Book for Children 1998, numerous other awards

  From Tadpole to Frog. HarperCollins, 1994, ISBN 0060230444, American Booksellers Association Pick of the Lists, *Science Books & Film Magazine*'s Best Children's Science Books of 1994

- Requirements: Two tables

Kimanne Smith

92 Independence Avenue
Wayne, NJ 07470
(973) 839-4882
smithki@wpunj.edu

Kimanne Smith shows samples of her work and her books, and talks about the process of illustrating a book.

- Grade levels: K-12

- $

- *Mary Ann Shadd Cary.* Lerner, forthcoming

  Prudence Crandall. Lerner, 2001, ISBN 1575054809

  The Canning Season. Carolrhoda, 1999, ISBN 1575052601

Pamela Curtis Swallow

75 Summer Road
Flemington, NJ 08822
(908) 788-7884
(908) 284-2026 fax
Pam@PamelaCurtisSwallow.com
bird@blast.net
<www.PamelaCurtisSwallow.com>

Pam Swallow's slide presentation takes students behind the scenes of how her books were made, and allow kids a look at how she lives and works. With Pam's encouragement, students learn how to turn everyday life into rich story material and are motivated to develop characters, setting, and plot.

- Grade levels: K-12

- $$

- *A Whistle Pig Is a Woodchuck Is a Groundhog.* Putnam, forthcoming

  A Writer's Notebook. Scholastic, 1999, ISBN 0590149695

  Wading Through Peanut Butter. Scholastic, 1993, ISBN 0590457934

Thomas F. Yezerski

270 Union Avenue, #6C
Rutherford, NJ 07070
(201) 939-6093 phone/fax
thomasfyezerski@worldnet.att.net
<home.att.net/~thomasfyezerski>

 See how a kid who loved to write and draw grew up to be an author and illustrator. Thomas Yezerski talks with students about their reading, writing, and drawing experiences and compares them to what he does every day in the "funnest" job in the whole world. His fast-paced slide presentation shows kids his progress from first drawing in kindergarten up to (and past) those nasty rejection letters. Highlights include slides of his third-grade homework; embarrassing pictures of his family; a real editor; and revisions, revisions, revisions.

- Grade levels: K-6

- $$

- *A Full Hand.* Farrar, Straus & Giroux, 2002, ISBN 0374425027

  Queen of the World. Farrar, Straus & Giroux, 2000, ISBN 037436 1657, Bank Street Books Best Children's Books of the Year

  Together in Pinecone Patch. Farrar, Straus & Giroux, 1998, ISBN 0374376476, Riverbank Review Children's Book of Distinction, National Council for Social Studies/Children's Book Council Notable, Living the Dream Award nominee

- Requirements: Slide projector, microphone

New York

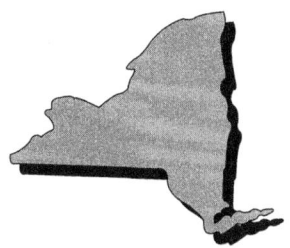

David A. Adler

c/o Holiday House
425 Madison Avenue
New York, NY 10017
(212) 688-0085
CAMJ563@aol.com
<www.davidaadler.com>

David Adler's presentation follows a book from idea through research, writing, rewriting, editing, galleys, illustration, and printing. He often shows students manuscript pages and compares those pages to the finished page to show kids how drastic his rewrites are. He's the author of more than 150 books.

- Grade levels: K-6
- $$$
- *The Cam Jansen Mystery* series. Viking, various ISBNs

  The Picture Book Biography series. Holiday House, various ISBNs

  The Andy Russell Books. Harcourt Brace, various ISBNs

Selina Alko

656 Carroll Street, #2-L
Brooklyn, NY 11215
(718) 768-8133 phone/fax
alcolors@aol.com
<www.selinaalko.com>

Selina Alko's innovative, clear presentation explains the creation of her children's book illustrations, from thumbnail sketches to bound books. She uses storyboards, pictures, and diagrams, and gives insight into her finished art, which features collage, gouache paint, and mixed media.

- Grade levels: K-3
- $
- *The God Around Us.* By Mira Brechto, UAHC Press, 1998, ISBN 0807407011, 087407380 pbk

Carol Barkin

47 Villard Avenue
Hastings-on-Hudson, NY 10706
(914) 478-0612
(914) 478-3860 fax
Cbark1@aol.com

Carol Barkin has collaborated with writing partner Elizabeth James on more than 35 books. In her presentations, she reveals how they became a team and how the partnership works across 3,000 miles. She also talks about how an idea becomes a book, using real-life examples.

- Grade levels: 3-6
- $$
- *School Survival Guide* series. HarperCollins, various ISBNs

  New Complete Babysitter's Handbook. Clarion, 1995, ISBN 0395665574, 0395665582 pbk

  The Holiday Handbook. Clarion, 1994, ISBN 0395650119, 0395678889 pbk

Kathleen Bart

1930-17 Sunrise Highway
Merrick, NY 11566
(516) 546-4919
teddybearbook@aol.com
<www.twoteddies.com>

 Travel back in time with author/illustrator Kathleen Bart to learn the true story of how the teddy bear came to be. Two teddy bears were created at the same time 100 years ago—and each "claims" to be the first. Kathleen presents each bear's side of the argument through engaging narrative and poster-sized illustrations. After the bears' lively debate, the audience must decide which one was truly first. Kathleen concludes the program by demonstrating the steps involved in writing and illustrating a picture book.

- Grade levels: K-6

- $$

- *A Tale of Two Teddies.* Portfolio Press, 2001, ISBN 0942620518

Susan Williams Beckhorn

195 Irish Hill Road
Rexville, NY 14877
(607) 356-3154
susb@infoblvd.net

Susan Beckhorn gets kids writing with her presentation on *A Writer's Toolbox: It's Not Just Paper and Pencils.* Students encounter surprising things in her toolbox: a rubber caterpillar (the bookworm that tells her that a writer reads), a troll-jar, a compass, blueprints, a saw, X-ray glasses, earphones, and butt glue. Using animal myths as a starting place, Susan's workshop inspires kids to write and teaches them how to critique and revise in a positive manner.

- Grade levels: 3-8

- $

- *The Kingfisher's Gift.* Philomel, 2002, ISBN 0399237127

  In the Morning of the World: Six Woodland Stories. Down East Books, 2000, ISBN 0892725036

- Requirements: Lapel microphone

Timothy D. Bellavia

230 East 25th Street, #2E
New York, NY 10010
(212) 685-8632 phone/fax
Tools4tolerance@aol.com
<www.weareallthesameinside.com>

 Author and artist Timothy D. Bellavia works with students by reading his highly acclaimed picture book *We Are All the Same Inside* and making Sage Dolls (the main character from the story), which children can dress and decorate with their own designs. His book and products are designed to help youngsters explore issues surrounding diversity of race, culture, religion, and gender, while giving them tools of tolerance and acceptance.

- Grade levels: K-6

- $

- *Come and Abide, We Are All the Same Inside.* T.I.M.M.-E Co., 2002, ISBN pending

  We Are All The Same Inside. T.I.M.M.-E Co., 2000, ISBN 0615113958

- Requirements: Slide projector, TV/VCR

Judy Bradbury

90 Wellingwood Drive
East Amherst, NY 14051-1743
(716) 688-0384
judywrites@yahoo.com

Judy Bradbury details what authors do all day in her presentation and uses participating students' work, along with that of noted authors, to demonstrate key elements of memorable writing.

- Grade levels: 5-8

- $$

- *Doggone Lemonade Stand!* McGraw-Hill, 1999, ISBN 0070070423

  Double Bubble Trouble! McGraw-Hill, 1998, ISBN 0070070407

  One Carton of Oops! McGraw-Hill, 1997, ISBN 00700703903

- Requirements: Slide projector, screen, overhead projector

Patience Brewster

3872 Jordan Road
Skaneateles, NY 13152
(315) 685-3540
(315) 685-5713 fax
patinabee@aol.com

Patience Brewster talks about stretching the imagination to keep it alive and fit. She shows students slides of artwork that she created by stretching her own imagination around past experiences and shares her process of working, from making sketches and generating thoughts to having finished books. She's illustrated more than 30 books and has won numerous awards, and her work appears in many collections and magazines. She's also designed puzzles, greeting cards, rubber stamps, and Christmas ornaments.

- Grade levels: K-12
- $$$
- *The Merbaby.* Holiday House, 2001, ISBN 0823415317

  Pee Wee's Tale. North-South Books, 2000, ISBN 15871710272

  Too Many Puppies. Scholastic, 1997, ISBN 0590602764
- Requirements: Carousel slide projector, large pad of paper, easel

Janis Brody

70 East 10th Street, Apt. 20E
New York, NY 10003
JanisBBrody@cs.com
<www.GurlThang.com>

Janis Brody, a clinical psychologist who specializes in adolescent development, leads workshops for young people based on her books. She focuses on topics such as developing a positive body image, puberty, romance, self-esteem, nutrition, eating disorders, sports, competition, and drugs. She speaks fearlessly to males and females and knows how to keep the discussion lively by presenting personalized quizzes and fun facts, and discussing kids' questions.

- Grade levels: 6-12
- $
- *Your Body: The Girl's Guide.* St. Martin's Press, 2000, ISBN 0312975635

  Bringing Home the Laundry: Effective Parenting for College and Beyond. Taylor Publishing, 2000, ISBN 08783301840

James Bruchac

23 Middle Grove Road
Greenfield Center, NY 12833
(518) 583-9980
asban@earthlink.net
<www.ndakinna.com>

Professional tracker, Adirondack guide, naturalist, writer, and storyteller Jim Bruchac grew up hearing the traditional American Indian stories of his Abenaki father, Joe Bruchac. For the last 10 years Jim's been bringing his lively combination of Native American storytelling, wilderness skills, and awareness of the natural world to appreciative audiences throughout the U.S. His school and library programs include everything from tall tales, American Indian games, Native songs and lore, and animal tracking to writing and storytelling workshops.

- Grade levels: K-12
- $$
- *How Chipmunk Got His Stripes.* Dial, 2001, ISBN 0803724047, Junior Library Guild selection

  Scats and Tracks of the Northeast. Falcon, 2001, ISBN 158592105x

  When the Chenoo Howls: Native American Monster Stories. Walker, 1998, ISBN 0802775764

Joseph Bruchac

PO Box 308
Greenfield Center, NY 12833
(518) 584-1728
(518) 583-9741 fax
nudatlog@earthlink.net
<www.josephbruchac.com>

Joseph Bruchac's programs combine storytelling, Native American music (he plays flute and drums, and sings traditional Abenaki songs), and discussion of his writing. He received a Lifetime Achievement Award from the Native Writers Circle of the Americas in 1999 and was named Storyteller of the Year by the Woodcraft Circle of Native writers and storytellers in 1998.

- Grade levels: K-12
- $$$
- *Bowman's Store: A Journey to Myself.* Lee & Low, 2001, ISBN 1584300272

  Skeleton Man. HarperCollins, 2001, ISBN 0060290757

  Sacajawea. Scholastic, 2000, ISBN 0-439280680

Stephanie Calmenson

205 East 22nd Street, #3L
New York, NY 10010
(212) 725-4280 fax
sc242@hotmail.com

Stephanie Calmenson's funny and informative slide presentation explores the making of a book, from idea to publication, and working with artists, co-authors, and editors. She discusses a visit with an editor at a major New York publishing house and reads from her work. She also offers a slide show featuring her dog Rosie (the star of *Rosie, a Visiting Dog's Story*).

- Grade levels: Adult (prefers to speak at teacher/library conferences)
- $$
- *Good For You! Toddler Rhymes for Toddler Times.* HarperCollins, 2001, ISBN 0688177379

  Perfect Puppy. Clarion, 2001, ISBN 0618011390

  The Frog Principal. Scholastic, 2001, ISBN 0590370707

- Requirements: Carousel slide projector, microphone

Alyssa Satin Capucilli

29 Windsor Road
Hastings-on-Hudson, NY 10706
(914) 478-1899
(914) 478-7168 fax
acapucilli@aol.com
<www.alyssacapucilli.com>

Read with Me, Write with Me, beckons Alyssa Capucilli, author of the *Biscuit* series, who believes we all have stories to share and tell. In order to invite, excite, and inspire students to enter the irresistible world of storytelling, she shares with them what it's like to be an author, how images and ideas weave their way into books, and how a book gets published. Her presentations include a slide show, puppetry, and storytelling, along with oversize prototypes of her books.

- Grade levels: K-2
- $$-$$$
- *Mrs. McTats and Her Houseful of Cats.* McElderry, 2001, ISBN 0689831854

  Biscuit's New Trick. HarperCollins, 2000, ISBN 00660280670, Oppenheim Gold Award

  Bathtime for Biscuit. HarperCollins, 1999, ISBN 0060279370, Garden State Children's Book Award, American Booksellers Association Pick of the Lists

Judith Caseley

32 Coolidge Avenue
Glen Head, NY 11545
jcaseley@aol.com
<www.judithcaseley.com>

Judith Caseley's motivational, entertaining presentation includes anecdotal speeches, a slide show, and a drawing she makes for students that describes the circuitous route of her career. She was a greeting card designer who was told "you'll never become a children's illustrator"—and went on to become an author and illustrator of more than 30 books.

- Grade levels: K-6
- $$$
- *On the Town: A Community Adventure.* Greenwillow, 2002, ISBN 0-06-029584-8

Bully. Greenwillow, 2001, ISBN 0688178677

Field Day Friday. Greenwillow, 2000, ISBN 0688167616

- Requirements: Slide projector, easel, paper, sound system

Yangsook Choi

106 East 31st Street, #2B
New York, NY 10016
(212) 684-0073
koalatale@yahoo.com
<www.yangsookchoi.com>

Yangsook Choi's programs take students into the creative process of book making, including getting an idea, writing, storyboarding, and illustrating. She shows each stage of the process through original sketchbooks, printer's proofs, and paintings, as well as drawing demonstrations.

- Grade levels: K-12
- $$
- *The Name Jar.* Knopf, 2001, ISBN 037580613x

  Rice Is Life. Henry Holt, 2000, ISBN 0805057196

  New Cat. Farrar, Straus & Giroux, 1999, ISBN 0374355126
- Requirements: Easel, large drawing pad, markers, display easels

Jill Clayson and Genia Miller

Backtalk Productions
PO Box 393
Rifton, NY 12471
(845) 658-3942
Backtalk01@aol.com

Backtalk Productions, a.k.a. Jill Clayson and Genia Miller, presents original, award-winning scripts from the perspective of those who lived "back then" (in 18th- and 19th-century America) to capture the spirit of the times and the people. The duo customizes living history to the needs of your school, but current offerings include *My Dear Son*, featuring two mothers (one Northern, one Southern) who meet at Gettysburg; *The Generals' Misses,* in which Mrs. Robert E. Lee and Mrs. Ulysses S. Grant read battlefield letters from their husbands; and *Molly Was No Lady*, which showcases the Industrial Revolution labor struggles of the Molly Macguires.

- Grade levels: K-12
- $
- Requirements: Two slide projectors

Rita Cleary

20 Cove Woods Road
Oyster Bay, NY 11771
(516) 922-1672
(516) 922-1713 fax
rmcleary@mindspring.com
<www.RitaCleary.com>

 A former teacher turned writer of historical novels, Rita Cleary presents a slide show about her various books.

- Grade levels: K-12
- $$
- *Spies and Tories.* Sunstone, 2001, ISBN 0865343241

  Sorrell. Sunstone, 2001, ISBN 0865341915

  RiverWalk. Five Star, 2000, ISBN 0786218452

Jehan Clements

PO Box 543
Tarrytown, NY 10591
(914) 366-7881
storyteller8@earthlink.net
<www.storytellercompany.com>

In addition to a program of traditional stories from around the world, Jehan Clements offers creative writing and book-making workshops featuring a patented *My Very Own Do-it-Yourself Storytelling Flip-over Picture Book.*

- Grade levels: K-6
- $
- *Alfred the Ant.* Storyteller Company, 2001, ISBN 0962250007
- Requirements: Two chairs

Vicki Cobb

302 Pondside Drive
White Plains, NY 10607
(914) 949-1104
(914) 949-1977 fax
email@vickicobb.com
<www.vickicobb.com>

This noted author shares with kids intriguing information and great science activity ideas. Vicki Cobb is the recipient of the Eve Gordon Award for contribution to children's science literature, the American Library Association Pick of the List, the Outstanding Science Trade Books, a Parents' Choice, the American Booksellers Association Pick of the List, and the New York Academy of Science Best Science Book of the Year Award. She encourages kids to read more about her in the *Grandmothers at Work* series title *Meet My Grandmother: She's a Children's Book Author* by Lisa McElroy with a little help from Abigail Jane Cobb.

- Grade levels: K-8 (but prefers middle grades)

- $$$

- *Open Your Eyes: Discovering Your Sense of Sight.* Millbrook, 2002, ISBN 0761317958

  See for Yourself: More Than 100 Experiments for Science Fairs and Projects. Scholastic, 2001, ISBN 0439090105

  Science Experiments You Can Eat. HarperCollins, 1994, ISBN 0064460029

- Requirements: Materials for demonstration (she'll provide details)

Caron Lee Cohen

508 East 78th Street, #4P
New York, NY 10021
(212) 628-9800
caronleecohen@earthlink.net

Caron Cohen's *Let's Make a Story* workshop for younger students features playful props, such as a ball, blocks, and balloons, to help kids create a story. Her *Courage and Coping with Fear* workshop includes a Native American tale and other pieces, followed by discussion to compare how they represent fear, courage, and heroism, to show students how themes in stories reflect universal needs in an increasingly complex world. Caron stresses research, revision, and self-acceptance as the writer's tools.

- Grade levels: K-6

- $

- *Happy to You!* Illustrated by Rosanne Litzinger, Clarion, 2001, ISBN 0618042296

  How Many Fish? Illustrated by S. D. Schindler, HarperCollins, 1998, ISBN 0060277130

  The Mud Pony. Illustrated by Shonto Begay, Scholastic, 1989, ISBN 0590415263, a Reading Rainbow title, also available in Big Book and audio formats and in Spanish

James Lincoln Collier

c/o Scholastic Books
Stephanie Wimmer
(212) 389-3063 fax
SWimmer@scholastic.com

James Collier tells kids his reasons for becoming a writer, then leads a discussion of techniques to help students write easier and faster by using mental and emotional approaches to writing. James has won the Christopher Award, Newbery Honors, the National Book Award, and many more.

- Grade levels: 5-7

- $$$

- *War Comes to Willy Freeman.* Yearling, 1987, ISBN 0440495040

  My Brother Sam Is Dead. Simon & Schuster, 1984 reissue, ISBN 0027229807

  The Teddy Bear Habit. Dell, 1981, ISBN 0440485606

Shana Corey

573 2nd Street, #13
Brooklyn, NY 11215
(718) 369-2471

Shana Corey loves talking to kids about ideas and inspirations, and showing them the stages that her story goes through to become a book. In talks for older students, she emphasizes role models, fairness, and how one person can change the world.

- Grade levels: 1-4
- $$
- *Ballerina Bear.* Random House, 2002, ISBN 0375815167

  First Graders from Mars: Horus's Horrible Day. Scholastic, 2001, ISBN 0439262208, Junior Library Guild selection

  You Forgot Your Skirt, Amelia Bloomer! Scholastic, 2000, ISBN 0439078199, *Publishers Weekly* Flying Start Award, *Publishers Weekly* Best Children's Books, *Booklist* Editors Choice, *Parenting Magazine* Reading Magic Award
- Requirements: Overhead projector

Laurie Ann Crompton

105 Michigan Street
Long Beach, NY 11561
(516) 670-0566
Libertiann@aol.com

Laurie Ann Crompton speaks to junior and senior high school students about body-image awareness and self-acceptance. She advocates against the starvation imagery often found in the media and is dedicated to educating young people about the potentially harmful effects of anorexia and bulimia, as well as teaching them, ultimately, to love their natural bodies.

- Grade levels: 3-12
- $

Margaret Cusack

124 Hoyt Street, Boerum Hill
Brooklyn, NY 11217-2215
(718) 237-0145
(718) 237-2430 fax
cusackart@aol.com

Margaret Cusack's Norman Rockwell-type realist style is created with stitchery and fabric and has been used on posters, puzzles, children's books, and everything from a Broadway show advertisement to a U.S. postage stamp. She shows students how an illustration happens, from the initial sketch to the finished artwork. Margaret has won many art and illustration awards.

- Grade levels: K-12
- $$
- *My Family Quilt.* Harcourt, 2002, forthcoming

  The Christmas Carol Sampler. Harcourt Brace Jovanovich, 1983, ISBN 0152177523
- Requirements: Slide projector and table

Lorna McDonald Czarnota

PO Box 1641
Buffalo, NY 14215
(716) 837-0551
Lczarnota@aol.com

Lorna Czarnota is a professional storyteller, a musician, an artist, and an educator whose programs include traditional and original folktales, as well as hands-on historical workshops in medieval and colonial American studies. She's codirector of the Western New York Storytelling Institute and president of Crossroads, a not-for-profit organization specializing in bringing stories of choice and empowerment to troubled teens.

- Grade levels: K-12
- $

Teri Daniels

2075 Vine Drive
Merrick, NY 11566
Teri@teridanielsbooks.com
<www.teridanielsbooks.com>

Teri Daniels shares the wonder and fun of picture-book making with kids through amusing antics that simplify the four-color printing process and bold visuals that encourage youngsters to use writing tools that shape inspiration into publication. Music, humor, and props are used to explore the mysteries of naming characters, creating a perfect picture-book plot, and making rhyme work. Teri also offers a brainstorm session for older students and a session that explores the most common fiction formulas.

- Grade levels: K-6
- $$

Math Man. Orchard, 2001, ISBN 0439293081

Just Enough. Viking, 2000, ISBN 0670888737, *Riverbank Review*'s Children's Books of Distinction Award nominee

The Feet in the Gym. Winslow Press, 1999, ISBN 1890817120

- Requirements: Three tables, easel, CD player

Gibbs Davis

340 East 52nd Street, Apt. 7G
New York, NY 10022
(212) 371-5538 phone/fax
gibbsdavis@juno.com

Gibbs Davis offers a writing workshop that mixes mystery and history by building on one of her books set in the White House. Kids learn, through writing exercises, about the "magic of mysteries," then outline mysteries based on the president of their choice. They also learn the basics of Gibbs' "rules to write by," which have stood her in good stead through almost two dozen books.

- Grade levels: 3-6

- $

- *Camp Sink or Swim.* Random House, 1997, ISBN 0679982167

  White House Ghosthunters series. Simon & Schuster, 1996, ISBN 0671568558

  The Other Emily. Houghton Mifflin, 1984, ISBN 0-395549477

Pleasant DeSpain

405 Third Street, #2
Troy, NY 12180
(518) 271-1650
pleasant@worldnet.att.net
<www.youngauthor.com>

Author and storyteller Pleasant DeSpain educates and celebrates young authors with a variety of programs. *Pleasant Journeys* (storytelling) is comprised of true tales about reading and writing interwoven with tales about risk, fun, and adventure; *An Eight-Point Plan for Young Authors* engages imaginations and practical skills by using colorful charts, stories, and examples; *A Five-Point Plan for Very Young Authors* features a simple road map for story making.

- Grade levels: K-6

- $$

- *Sweet Land of Story: 36 American Stories to Tell.* August House, 2000, ISBN 087483569x

  The Emerald Lizard: 15 Latin American Tales to Tell in English and Spanish. August House, 1999, ISBN 0874835518

Carolyn Watson Dubisch

15 Sieber Road
Kerhonkson, NY 12446
(845) 626-4386 phone/fax
fanvisions@aol.com

Artist Carolyn Dubish helps children experience what it's like to illustrate a story that they helped write. She also teaches older children how to draw a face with character and expression.

- Grade levels: K-6

- $

- *Andy! And the Flying Toaster Tangerine.* Pentland Press, 2001, ISBN 1571972641

  The Giant's Playground. Armadillo Press, 2001, ISBN 0971474001

- Requirements: Pencils, colored pencils

Edward Einhorn

235 West 102nd Street, Apt. 16-S
New York, NY 10025
(212) 866-1073 phone/fax
utc61@hotmail.com
<www.untitledtheater.com/Paradox.html>

In his presentation called *Child Authors of Oz,* Edward Einhorn creates with students a story that combines elements of the Oz books with the kids' imaginations to produce a new fable. Edward's program utilizes his background as a writer and director to guide students through the creative process. He has directed numerous off-off-Broadway shows, including *The Living Methuselah* and *Ionesco's Tales for Children Less Than Three Years Old.*

- Grade levels: 3-12
- $$
- *Living House of Oz.* Hungry Tiger Press, forthcoming

  Paradox in Oz. Hungry Tiger Press, 2000, ISBN 1929527012

Katie Davis

Bedford Hills, NY 10507
(914) 244-8777 phone/fax
Katie@katiedavis.com
<www.katiedavis.com>

As the audience helps Katie Davis write a story, she invites participants to demonstrate emotional expressions that are used to create a new narrative with an emphasis on a beginning, a middle, and an end. Katie also uses visuals, such as overheads, posters, original art, early sketches, and book dummies. She also can bring a slide show or a PowerPoint presentation.

- Grade levels: K-6
- $$
- *Party Animals.* Harcourt, 2002, ISBN 015216670

  I Hate to Go To Bed. Harcourt Brace, 1999, ISBN 0152019200, Children's Book Council Children's Choice for 2000

  Who Hops? Harcourt Brace, 1998, ISBN 0152018395, National Parenting Publications Honor Award, Oppenheim Toy Portfolio Platinum Award
- Requirements: Overhead projector or easel with large pad or PowerPoint setup

Harriet K. Feder

132 Wickham Drive
Williamsville, NY 14221
(716) 634-8697 phone/fax
khkw@aol.com

Harriet gives a mini writing workshop on fiction and nonfiction in which students participate by discussing, questioning, and ultimately writing outlines of their own projected work. Those who are interested in publishing are given lists of publications that accept student writing.

- Grade levels: 6-12
- $$
- *Death on Sacred Ground.* Lerner, 2001, ISBN 0822507412, Edgar Young Adult nominee

  Mystery of the Kaifeng Scroll. Lerner, 1995, ISBN 0822507390

  Mystery in Miami Beach. Lerner, 1992, ISBN 0822507331

Betsy Franco Feeney

103 Massachusetts Avenue
Congers, NY 10920
(845) 268-2592
(845) 268-9278 fax
BetsFeeney@aol.com
<www.theispot.com/artist/feeney>

Betsy Feeney takes students on a visual journey of creativity, from earliest imaginative sketches through finished watercolors and final books, by using slides from two books she illustrated. Students also can learn to design and illustrate their own writing by using the principles of good design that Betsy shares with them.

- Grade levels: K-12
- $
- *Party.* Harcourt Brace, 2001, ISBN 0153277742

  James Bear and the Goose Gathering. Scribners, 1994, ISBN 0684195267
- Requirements: Two tables, slide projector cart, microphone, easel

Constance Foland

175 West 87th Street, Apt. 18-D
New York, NY 10024
CMF131@aol.com

Using examples from her books, Constance Foland teaches students about writing poems, entering ideas in journals, and bringing characters to life.

- Grade levels: 3-6
- $

Flying High Pogo. Pleasant Company, 2002, forthcoming

A Song for Jeffrey. Pleasant Company, 1999, ISBN 1562478494

- Requirements: TV/VCR, overhead projector

Nancy Furstinger

48 Loyola Road
Elizaville, NY 12523
(845) 756-3174
nancyf@webjogger.net

Albert Einstein said, "Our task must be to free ourselves by widening our circle of compassion to embrace all living creatures and the whole of nature in its beauty." Nancy Furstinger instills in kids a sense of love and respect for all creatures through a combination of animal books, crafts, and live pets.

- Grade levels: 2-7
- $

Creative Crafts for Critters. Stoddart Kids, 2001, ISBN 0773761357

From Sea to Shining Sea: Connecticut. Grolier, 2001, ISBN 0516223240

Fun Stuff with Your Best Friend: The Interactive Dog Book. Doral Publishing, 2000, ISBN 0944875661

Melanie Hope Greenberg

168 Hicks Street
Brooklyn, NY 11201
(718) 522-7026 phone/fax
melhopegreenberg@aol.com

 Melanie Greenberg's workshop on the author-illustrator process takes students from original story concept through creating the rough dummy to finished art and the final printing. She uses slides to show students how her book ideas got onto a bookshelf as picture books.

- Grade levels: K-6
- $$

The Wind's Garden. By Bethany Roberts, Henry Holt, 2001, ISBN 0805063676

Supermarket! By Kathleen Krull, Holiday House, 2001, ISBN 0823415465

Down in the Subway. By Miriam Cohen, DK Ink, 1998, ISBN 0789425106, National Council for Social Studies Notable Social Studies Books for Young People

- Requirements: Slide projector, screen, microphone, large paper, easel, markers

Dan Greenburg

645 North Broadway, #16
Hastings-on-Hudson, NY 10706
(914) 478-0382 phone/fax
dan.greenburg@verizon.net

Dan Greenburg gets students, especially reluctant readers, excited about books and writing. Drawing on his performing background, he reads from his books in character voices, tells kids how he became a writer, and explains why it's the best job in the world. He also tells them how he gets ideas and shows them how to develop their own ideas into an outline, then a story, then a book. Dan says his many adventures—including exploring live volcanoes, teaching dolphins, searching for the Loch Ness monster, exploring supernatural phenomena, hanging out with cops and firefighters, and training lions and tigers—usually end up as books.

- Grade levels: 2-5
- $$

The Zack Files series. Penguin Putnam (24 in print, 4 more coming), various ISBNs

The Maximum Boy series. Scholastic, (4 in print, 2 more coming), various ISBNs

Judith Greenburg (J. C. Greenburg)

16 River Glen
Hastings-on-Hudson, NY 10706
(914) 478-7241
(914) 478-0382 fax
Will.green@verizon.net
<www.AndrewLost.com>

Judith Greenburg's *Andrew Lost* stories are like Indiana Jones meets *Honey, I Shrunk the Kids*, with the hero adventuring through squishy, oozy, prickly, crawly, smelly, watery worlds of science. Her classroom visits bring these ideas alive for young readers by featuring spectacular electron micrographs of flies' feet, ants' eyes, and spiders' spinnerets that illustrate how living things work. She also gives hands-on demos, such as making huge bubbles to introduce the properties of water. At each point in her program, she helps audiences enter the process of writing descriptively, accurately, and imaginatively.

- Grade levels: 2-3
- $$

- *Andrew Lost: On the Dog.* Random House, 2002, ISBN 0375812776

  Andrew Lost: In the Bathroom. Random House, 2002, ISBN 0375912789

  Andrew Lost: In the Kitchen. Random House, 2002, ISBN 0375812792

- Requirements: Screen, microphone

Elaine Greenstein

521 2nd Street
Brooklyn, NY 11215
(718) 499-5607
elainegreenstein@aol.com

Eleven years ago, Elaine Greenstein never even imagined she would write a book—now she's working on her 10th, which is about the invention of ice cream cones. She shares with students her experiences as a writer and illustrator, telling them stories and showing them original art from her books. Using a portable etching press, she discusses the stages of making her books, from idea, imagination, writing, and revising to how they're printed. She also leads workshops on book binding and setting up a publishing center in the classroom.

- Grade levels: K-12
- $$

- *As Big as You.* Knopf, 2002, ISBN 0375813535

  Dreaming. Scholastic, 2001, ISBN 0439063027

  The Mitten Tree. Fulcrum, 1999, ISBN 1555913490

Elizabeth Hall

PO Box 4
Waccabuc, NY 10597
(914) 763-1148 fax
Eunice@cloud9.net

Elizabeth Hall, author of nine children's books and widow of Newbery and Hans Christian Andersen prize-winning author Scott O'Dell, shows children how books go from an idea in an author's head to a published novel. Using photos, videotape, samples of cover art, and samples of writing from manuscript to printed page, she brings excitement to the research and writing process. Writing comes alive when children hear about encounters with dolphins, scuba-diving, meetings with wolves, and low flights over snow-clad Alaskan mountains. Elizabeth chats informally with children about the writing of Scott's books and her own.

- Grade levels: 3-6
- $

- *Child of the Wolves.* Houghton Mifflin, 1996, ISBN 0395765021, 0440413214 pbk, Junior Library Guild selection, Maud Hart Lovelace Award nominee, Children's Crown Classic Book 1999

  Venus Among the Fishes. Houghton Mifflin, 1995, ISBN 0395705614, 0440411750 pbk, Tennessee State Award nominee

  Thunder Rolling in the Mountains. Houghton Mifflin, 1992, ISBN 0395599660, 0440408792 pbk, Children's Trade Book in the field of Social Studies notable 1992, South Carolina Junior Book Award nominee

- Requirements: TV/VCR

Jim Haskins

325 West End Avenue, 7D
New York, NY 10023
(212) 873-4852
(212) 873-4853 fax
Jsh1nyc@aol.com

Jim Haskins has dozens and dozens of books in print, whose topics range from the Underground Railroad to break dancing. He speaks to students about the process of writing and discusses any of the topics in his books.

- Grade levels: K-12
- $
- *Count Your Way* series. Lerner, various ISBNs

Marianna Heusler

304 East 65th Street, #8B
New York, NY 10021
(212) 396-1561
henridge@aol.com
<www.mariannamystery.com>

Marianna Heusler talks with kids about the good and bad aspects of the writing life, as well as the components of a well-written mystery story. She reads from *The Night the Penningtons Vanished*, then gives students an assignment and awards a prize for the best mini-story.

- Grade levels: 5-8
- $
- *The Night the Penningtons Vanished*. Larcom Press, 2002, ISBN 0971437009

Jennifer Holm

dearmay@crowdedfire.com
<www.jenniferholm.com>

Jennifer Holm emphasizes the importance of personal history as inspiration in her presentations. She discusses how she goes about writing a book, from initial idea through research, writing, revision, editorial changes, and finally to publication. She shows kids how her childhood experiences contributed to plot points in her books to inspire and excite them about writing.

- Grade levels: 3-8
- $$$
- *Boston Jane.* HarperCollins, 2001, ISBN 0060287381

  Our Only May Amelia. HarperCollins, 1999, ISBN 0064408566, Newbery Honor Book, Parents' Choice Silver Award, *Publishers Weekly* Best Book of 1999

Johanna Hurwitz

10 Spruce Place
Great Neck, NY 11021
(516) 829-6205
imhur@yahoo.com (teachers only, please)

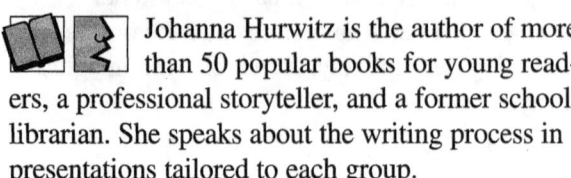

Johanna Hurwitz is the author of more than 50 popular books for young readers, a professional storyteller, and a former school librarian. She speaks about the writing process in presentations tailored to each group.

- Grade levels: K-12
- $$$
- *Russell's Secrets.* HarperCollins, 2001, ISBN 0688175740

  Class Clown. Scholastic, 1995, ISBN 0590418211

  The Hot & Cold Summer. Scholastic, 1991, ISBN 0590339448

Roberta Grobel Intrater

1212 Beverley Road
Brooklyn, NY 11218
(718) 462-4004
(718) 826-1396 fax
rgistudio@earthlink.net

Drawing on her background as a graphic designer, fine artist, and photographer, author Roberta Intrater's presentations include discussion of how a book is made and how to create a flip-book of class portraits, and a reading and discussion of *The Christmas Puppy*, a story of love, loss, difficult choices, and compassion.

- Grade levels: 1-12
- $$
- *Two Eyes, a Nose and a Mouth.* Cartwheel/Scholastic, 2000, ISBN 0439116805

  Peek-a-Boo, You! Cartwheel/Scholastic, 2002, ISBN 0439339618

  Awesome Art Activities Around the Year: 20 Dazzling Projects That Connect to Your Curriculum and Delight All Learners. Scholastic Professional Books, 2001, ISBN 0439044987

Marilyn Janovitz

41 Union Square West
New York, NY 10003
(212) 727-8330
(212) 267-2524 fax
mjanovitz@aol.com

 Author and illustrator Marilyn Janovitz engages, educates, and entertains students. She demonstrates how a picture book is made by turning an idea into a dummy, creating the finished art, then sharing uncut, printers' proof sheets and the final book with students. Using a big book version of *Look Out, Bird,* she talks about "circular stories." She also offers a drawing demo and challenges listeners to guess some of the many foreign language into which *Is It Time?* was translated.

- Grade levels: K-2
- $

Good Morning, Little Fox. North-South Books, 2001, ISBN 0735814406

Little Fox. North-South Books, 1999, ISBN 0735811601, 0735815704 pbk, 0735815730 (Spanish), 0735815747 pbk (Spanish)

Look Out, Bird! North-South Books, 1994, ISBN 1558582495, 1558587200 pbk, 1558587209 (Spanish), 1558587195 pbk (Spanish)

Marthe Jocelyn

552 Broadway
New York, NY 10012
(212) 431-0293 fax
Mmj8@aol.com

 Using her picture books illustrated with fabric collage, Marthe Jocelyn talks with kids about how a picture book is made, from the dummy sketches to the finished art, and briefly explains four-color printing. She also speaks to older students about where ideas come from, how to love rewriting, and how to do historical research.

- Grade levels: K-5
- $

Earthly Astonishments. Dutton, 2000, ISBN 0525462635, Canadian Library Association Book of the Year finalist

Hannah's Collections. Dutton, 2000, ISBN 0525464425, Governor General's Award for illustration

The Invisible Day. Puffin, 1997, ISBN 0141306416

Bobbi Katz

Port Emery, NY 12466
(914) 338-8163
bobbikatz@aol.com

 When Bobbi Katz visits schools, she uses her poetry to connect with the curriculum. She incorporates first-person poems, works for two or more readers, and for the youngest children, sounds such as school-bus noises and the hush of snow.

- Grade levels: K-12
- $$

A Rumpus of Rhymes: A Book of Noisy Poems. Illustrated by Susan Chwasz, Dutton, 2000, ISBN 0525667181

Sarah S. Kilborne

One Gramercy Park West
New York, NY 10003
Goodtown@aol.com

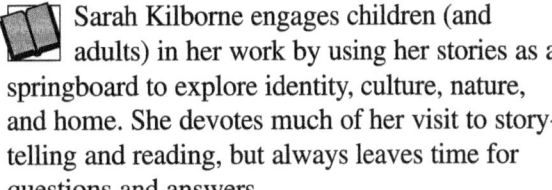 Sarah Kilborne engages children (and adults) in her work by using her stories as a springboard to explore identity, culture, nature, and home. She devotes much of her visit to storytelling and reading, but always leaves time for questions and answers.

- Grade levels: K-12
- $

Leaving Vietnam: The True Story of Tuan Ngo. Simon & Schuster, 1999, ISBN 068980797x, Junior Library Guild selection, *Booklist* starred review

Peach and Blue. Illustrated by Seven Johnson and Lou Fancher, Knopf, 1994, ISBN 0679890955, *Today Show* feature, *Washington Post* all-time favorite love story

Gordon Korman

4 Glamford Road
Great Neck, NY 11023
(516) 504-0747
(515) 504-0746 fax
info@gordonkorman.com or gkorman@optonline.net
<www.gordonkorman.com>

Gordon Korman's fast-moving, entertaining presentation centers around his first book, which was written as a seventh-grade language arts assignment and published by Scholastic two years later, when he was 14. Gordon discusses topics such as brainstorming, developing characters, dialogue, rewriting, revision, and of course, his trademark humor with students. Twenty-five years after that junior high project (*This Can't Be Happening at MacDonald Hall*), he has more than 40 books and numerous series in print and has won a slew of awards. He says, "I grew up, but my imagination was held back in the middle grades."

- Grade levels: 1-8

- $$$

- *Everest Trilogy* series. Scholastic, 2002, various ISBNs

  No More Dead Dogs. Hyperion, 2000, ISBN 0-786805315

- Requirements: Sound system for large groups

Steven Kroll

64 West 11th Street
New York, NY 10011
(212) 674-1768

 Steven Kroll offers an interactive slide presentation on how an idea becomes a book. He tells kids how he lives and works as a writer, how ideas for stories happen, and how ideas have developed into books. He shows slides of his street, his apartment, lions in Africa, and an elephant in India (with him on it), and he reads to students. He enjoys leading story-writing sessions as well as speaking.

- Grade levels: K-6

- $$$

- *Sweet America: An Immigrant's Story*. Jamestown Publishers, 2000, ISBN 0809206226

  By the Dawn's Early Light: The Story of the Star Spangled Banner. Scholastic, 1994, ISBN 0590450557

  The Biggest Pumpkin Ever. Cartwheel, 1993, ISBN 0590464639

- Requirements: Carousel slide projector, microphone

Karen Land

500 Meadow Lane
Cutchogue, NY 11935
(631) 734-5263
Klandbooks@aol.com
Land@greenport.k12.ny.us
<www.geocities.com/klandbooks>

Veteran storyteller Karen Land has appeared on NBC and CBS News promoting her *Read With Me—No TV* program and has developed a variety of toddler-time and Mother Goose story times for libraries. She's also created *Maria Alvarez*, a one-woman show based on her Hispanic Menorcan heritage, whose character lives in 18th-century Florida.

- Grade levels: K-12

- $$

Barbara Lanza

PO Box 118
Pine Island, NY 10969
(845) 258-4601
(845) 258-1241 fax
blanza@optonline.net
<www.creativehotlist.com/b_lanza>

 Barbara Lanza's lively presentation leaves participants with a greater understanding of the making of a picture book. Her program begins with her childhood love of fairy-tale heroines, which she depicts in pencil and crayon, and proceeds through showing page layouts from publishers' drawings, finished art, and printed books. She concludes with a description of the process, which unites editors, artists, and printers. Barbara has more than 30 books to her credit.

- Grade levels: K-12

- $$
- *Great Christmas Tree Celebration.* Scholastic, 2001, ISBN 0439282004
- *The Great Golden Easter Egg Hunt.* Scholastic, 2000, ISBN 043914268
- *Dearest Baby.* Western Publishing, 1993, ISBN 0307123944
- Requirements: Easel, slide projector

Marilyn Levinson

103 Maytime Drive
Jericho, NY 11753
(516) 935-4552
marilev@juno.com

In Marilyn Levinson's *Meet The Author* session, she shares her early experiences that led to her becoming a writer, reads from her novels, and explains how her characters sprang to life. She also speaks on the process of writing a novel and the publishing experience, using her novels as examples in a session entitled *An Author Talks about Writing.*

- Grade levels: 4-12
- $$
- *Rufus and Magic Run Amok.* Marshall Cavendish, 2001, ISBN 0761451021
- *And Don't Bring Jeremy.* iUniverse, 2001 (originally Holt, 1986), ISBN 0595169198
- *No Boys Allowed.* Troll/Bridgewater, 1993, ISBN 0816731357, Georgia Children's Book Award nominee

Star Livingstone

11946 State Route 28
Forestport, NY 13338
(315) 392-6104
starling@dreamscape.com

Through acting and games, Star Livingstone encourages children to use their creative imaginations and emphasizes the uniqueness of each student's vision. She also shares a story from her booktalks about story making and explains how a book is created.

- Grade levels: K-5

- $
- *Harley.* Seastar Books, 2001, ISBN 1587170485, American Library Association Notable Book

Hope Irvin Marston

PO Box 710
Black River, NY 13612-0710
(315) 773-5847
amarston@twcny.rr.com

Hope Marston has been visiting schools for 20 years to talk with kids about how they can get published. She engages them with her charming recounting of how she paints with words and why she writes for kids, and tells them tales of growing up on a Pennsylvania farm with eight siblings—and how she was always skinny. She uses toy vehicles and stuffed animals to help students relate to her past and her books.

- Grade levels: K-8
- $$
- *My Little Book of River Otters.* NorthWord Press, 1998, ISBN 1559716398
- *Wings in the Water: The Story of a Manta Ray.* Soundprints/Smithsonian, 1998, ISBN 1568995576
- *Fire Trucks.* Dutton/Cobblehill, 1996, ISBN 0525652310

Trish Marx

129 East 69th Street, #6C
New York, NY 10021
(212) 861-4361
pmarx34351@aol.com

Trish Marx takes students on a slide-show trip to a country currently in the news and shows them how to get their story, how to find their subject, what details to look for, what kinds of questions to ask, how to research, and how to turn it all into a book. Students learn about the history, geography, economy, and politics of the area "visited." More importantly, they learn about what it's like being a child in a difficult and dangerous place in the news.

- Grade levels: 4-7
- $-$$

Joy Masoff

14 Five Ponds Drive
Waccabuc, NY 10597
(914) 277-7722 ext. 3
(914) 277-7733 fax
Joy@webfields.com

Spend a day in a Colonial child's life with Joy Masoff's hands-on presentation featuring common classroom skills (kids make a facsimile hornbook) and punishments (from sapling nose-pinchers to crybaby signs that hung around a child's neck), as well as food tasting and games. Kids also can discover the truth about nasty things in a presentation called *Oh Yuck!* Or perhaps they'd rather meet the men and women of the fire and emergency world with Joy.

- Grade levels: 5-8

- $

- *Oh Yuck! The Encyclopedia of Everything Nasty.* Workman, 2000, ISBN 0761107711, New York Public Library Books for the Teen Age

  Chronicle of America: Colonial Times/American Revolution. Scholastic, 2000, ISBN 043905107, Notable Social Studies Trade Book

  Fire! Scholastic, 1998, ISBN 0590978721, American Library Association Quick Pick

Susan Rowan Masters

PO Box 97
Panama, NY 14767
(716) 782-4555 phone/fax
srmasters@madbbs.com
<www.madbbs.com/~srmasters>

Susan Masters offers workshops titled *Notebooks, Journals, and Memories* (hands-on exercises to help kids mine their own memories and enhance observational skills), *Writing Secrets You Can Use* (sharing some of her own secrets for good writing), *Poetry Pleasers* (designed to jump-start student creativity), and *Elements of Fiction* (a short guide to good writing).

- Grade levels: K-12

- $

Summer Song. Clarion, 1995, ISBN 0395712274

Libby Bloom. Henry Holt, 1995, ISBN 0805022742, Rhode Island Book Award nominee, Sequoyah Award Master List inclusion

The Secret Life of Hubie Hartzel. Lippincott, 1990, ISBN 0397323999

Anne Mazer

209 Willow Avenue
Ithaca, NY 14850
annemazer@yahoo.com

Anne Mazer, author of more than 20 books and an acclaimed series of anthologies, offers presentations that center on the love of reading and the process of writing. She speaks about growing up in a family of writers, how she began to write, developing ideas, rewriting and editing, and the relationship between writer and artist.

- Grade levels: K-6

- $$

- *The Salamander Room.* Illustrated by Steve Johnson, Knopf, 1991, ISBN 039482945x, ABC Children's Choice, Keystone to Reading Book Award, Reading Rainbow feature selection, American Booksellers Association Pick of the Lists

  The No-Nothings and Their Baby. Illustrated by Ross Collins, Scholastic, 2000, ISBN 0590680498

  The Oxboy. Persea Books, 2000, ISBN 0892552409, American Library Association Notable, National Council for Social Studies Notable Book

Ann McGovern

30 East 62nd Street
New York, NY
(212) 888-1962
amcgsch@aol.com
<www.AnnMcGovern.com>

One of the many reasons why Ann McGovern's presentations are so popular is her amazing diversity: She writes biography, history, nature, and adventure; retells folktales; and writes stories. She talks with kids about the inspirations for her books and her exotic travels to the Antarctic, the North Pole, the Galapagos, and Great Barrier Reef. Her slide shows are supplemented by anecdotes galore. Her purpose is to inspire love of reading and writing, and to share her craft.

- Grade levels: K-6
- $$$
- Requirements: Slide projector, microphone

Andy Morse (a.k.a. Andy the Music Man)
PO Box 357
Glenmont, NY 12077
(518) 462-3372
andysings@aol.com

Andy Morse is a children's musician who delights young audiences with a lively blend of sing-along, dancing, play-acting, and storytelling. A rhythmic guitarist, mandolin player, and songwriter, Andy takes great care to create an environment where children can comfortably participate. He's fluent in sign language and offers concerts, arts-in-education programs, and quality musical fun.

- Grade levels: K-3
- $

Roxie Munro
20 Park Avenue, #10-A
New York, NY 10016
(718) 706-0370 phone/fax
rxstudio@aol.com

Roxie Munro discusses with students the creation, research, and publishing process of her books, from idea through dummy to sketches, text, finished art, and edited copy, showing samples of each. Her school presentations also include giving each child a photocopy of a maze to solve and color. Sometimes she's accompanied by her husband, Bo Zaunders. Together, they read from *Crocodiles, Camels and Dugout Canoes* or *Feathers, Flaps and Flops* (which he wrote and she illustrated).

- Grade levels: K-12
- $$

Mazescapes. North-South Books, 2001, ISBN 1587170604, *School Library Journal* starred review, *Parenting Magazine* pick of the month

The Inside-Outside Book of Texas. North-South Books, 2001, ISBN 158717050

Feathers, Flaps and Flops: Fabulous Early Fliers. By Bo Zaunders, Dutton, 2001, ISBN 0525464662, *SLJ* starred review

- Requirements: Table, easel, slide projector

Aline Alexander Newman
RR 1 Box 43 East Road
Turin, NY 13473
(315) 348-6615 phone/fax
aanewman@aldus.northnet.org

Aline Newman lets students take the stage using wigs, hats, and other props, then flesh out their imaginary story people on paper. In her *Creative Captions* workshop, she shares guidelines for writing short, attention-grabbing captions, while in *My Life as a Writer*, she shows slides of herself as a child who dreamed of becoming a writer, then follows her funny, frustrating, but ultimately inspiring path to publication. She's also a freelance magazine writer with many publication credits, including caption writing for *National Geographic World*.

- Grade levels: 3-12
- $
- Requirements: Carousel slide projector w/remote, table

Josephine "Joi" Nobisso
602 Montauk Highway
Westhampton Beach, NY 11978
(631) 288-5119
(631) 288-5179 fax
ghbooks@optonline.net
<www.GingerbreadBooks.com>

Joi Nobisso offers students of all ages and skill levels innovative but accessible writing tips that instantly improve any written work, based on her experiences as an author, an editor, and a publishing professional. She also offers a slide program, *An Encounter with an Author, Editor, and Publisher,* to take students into the life of an author.

- Grade levels: K-12
- $$
- *Show, Don't Tell! Secrets of Writing.* Gingerbread House, 2002, ISBN 0940112132

  John Blair and the Great Hinckly Fire. Houghton Mifflin, 2000, ISBN 0618015604

  Hot Cha Cha! Winslow House, 1998, ISBN 1890817007
- Requirements: Slide projector

Marc Tyler Nobleman

(212) 661-2090
mtn@mtncartoons.com
<www.mtncartoons.com>

Marc Nobleman has written more than 20 books for young people, and he likes to share with students material that has a high "FQ" (fun quotient). His programs feature spelling, geography, and (his favorite) the Human Lie Detector Test, in which students pair up and reveal things about themselves, including deliberate lies—after which they must discriminate between fact and fib. Marc's been known to start a no-laughing contest and to recreate the Pony Express during his school visits.

- Grade levels: 4-7
- $
- *3-D Thrillers: Solar System.* Dutton, 2000, ISBN 0525464697

  365 Adventures. Dutton, 2000, ISBN 0525464972

  Felix Explores Our World. Abbeville, 1999, ISBN 0789205963

Julia Noonan

24 Bay Ridge Place
Brooklyn, NY 11209
(718) 748-4979
(718) 748-4018 fax
junoart@aol.com

Julia Noonan's art has been singled out for distinction from the beginning and has appeared in everything from *Good Housekeeping* to *Sesame Street Magazine.* She also has a large number of commercial artwork credits. In classrooms and libraries, however, she demonstrates the basics of storytelling by empowering her audience to choose a character, a setting, a problem to solve, and a resolution. Kids make it up as they go, and as their story unfolds, Julia illustrates it before their eyes. She also created a program called *By the Book,* in which professional writers and illustrators mentor students in creating their own novels and picture books.

- Grade levels: K-2
- $$
- *Bath Day.* Scholastic, 2000, ISBN 0439114926

  Breakfast Time. Scholastic, 2000, ISBN 043911490x

  Hare and Rabbit, Friends Forever. 2000, Scholastic, ISBN 0439087538
- Requirements: Blackboard or easel w/drawing pad

Linda Sue Park

c/o Clarion books, Marjorie Naughton
215 Park Avenue South
New York, NY 10003
(212) 420-5883
Marjorie_naughton@hmco.com
<www.lindasuepark.com>

Linda Sue Park offers booktalks or writing workshops for students that include a brief bio, storytelling (a Korean folktale), and a Korean clapping game. For older students she focuses on the writing and publishing process, from idea to finished book, paying special attention to the need for rewriting and revision.

- Grade levels: K-12
- $$
- *When My Name Was Keoko.* Clarion, 2002, ISBN 0618133356

  A Single Shard, Clarion, 2001, ISBN 0395978270, Newbery Medal, *Booklist* Editor's Choice, *School Library Journal* Best Book, New York Public Library 100 Titles for Reading and Sharing

  The Kite Fighters. Clarion, 2000, ISBN 0395940410

Helena Clare Pittman

820 Tanzman Road
Liberty, NY 12754

Helena Pittman has found that children are keenly interested in the mechanics of the process of writing and illustrating picture books. So, she shows them the works, from scribbly sketches through the interim stages to her finished paintings.

- Grade levels: 1-12
- $$
- Requirements: Table, microphone

Susanna Pitzer

946 Columbus Avenue, #3B
New York, NY 10025
(212) 932-9809
spitzer@nyc.rr.com

Susanna Pitzer's writing workshops include improvisational acting to create a story or play, drawing a clear story (even if you can't draw), and researching fiction based on fact by using periods of history turned into story. Produced plays include *Cinderella, the Grimm Sisters, Jemima Puddleduck, Monsters in the Closet,* and *Can You Hear the Talking Dog?*

- Grade levels: 2-7
- $
- *Grandfather Hurant Lives Forever.* Centering Corporation, 2001 ISBN 1561231592

Pam Pollack and Meg Belviso

117 West 74th Street, Apt. 3C
New York, NY 10023
(212) 875-1205
pdpollack@earthlink.net

Whenever this team talks to readers, the big question they're asked is, "How do you work together?" They share stories and examples from their work to find "funny" wherever it's hiding, and after sharing some pointers, they turn kids loose to try it with a partner of their own.

- Grade levels: K-6
- $

- *Malcolm in the Middle: The Bad Luck Charm.* Scholastic, 2001, ISBN 0439230780

- *Malcolm in the Middle: The Krelboyne Parrot.* Scholastic, 2001, ISBN 0439261333

- *Bear Cub.* Grosset & Dunlap, 2001, ISBN 0448425238

Doreen Rappaport

81 High View Farm Road
Copake Falls, NY 12517
(518) 325-7616
rapabook@aol.com
<www.doreenrappaport.com>

How do authors get ideas? Once they have ideas, how do they translate them into fiction and nonfiction? How do they plow through stumbling blocks and deal with criticism? Using examples from her 17 books, Doreen Rappaport opens the exciting process of writing, researching, thinking, and revising to students and empowers their writing.

- Grade levels: K-12
- $$
- *Martin's Big Words: The Life of Dr. Martin Luther King, Jr.* Illustrated by Bryan Collier, Hyperion, 2001, ISBN 0786807148, *Booklist* starred review, many awards

- *Freedom River.* Illustrated by Bryan Collier, Hyperion, 2000, ISBN 0786803509, Coretta Scott King honor book, American Library Association Notable

- *Dirt on Their Skirts: The Story of the Young Women Who Won the World Championship.* Illustrated by E. B. Lewis, Dial, 2000, ISBN 803720424, *School Library Journal* starred review

John H. Ritter

Author Appearance Coordinator
Penguin Putnam Books for Young Readers
345 Hudson Street, 15th Floor
New York, NY 10014
(212) 414-3468
(212) 414-3393 fax
Authorapp@penguinputnam.com
HeyJohn@JohnHRitter.com
<www.JohnHRitter.com>

Storyteller John H. Ritter's anecdote-filled program includes a slide show and is designed for audiences who've already read and studied his metaphorical, multilayered novels. His talk covers the humorous and sobering events of his boyhood, the difficult choices and moral dilemmas he's faced, and the decisions he's made, which have led him to writing his books. He hopes to inspire listeners to consider their own lives in order to follow their dreams. John's a winner of the Society of Children's Book Writers and Illustrators Judy Blume Award for 1994.

- Grade levels: 5-12

- $$-$$

- *Cruz Camacho: The Boy Who Saved Baseball.* Philomel, forthcoming

  Over the Wall. Philomel, 2000, ISBN 0399234896, Parents' Guide to Media Award, New York Public Library Books for the Teen Age, Texas State Library Lone Star Book

  Choosing Up Sides. Philomel, 1998, ISBN 0388231854, International Reading Association Children's Book Award, American Library Association Best Books for Young Adults, IRA Readers' Choice

- Requirements: Slide projector, lapel microphone, overhead projector

Miriam Schaer

199 Eighth Avenue, A3
Brooklyn, NY 11215
(718) 788-2029
(718) 788-0064 fax
mschaer@earthlink.net
<www.colphon.com/gallery/mschaer>

Miriam Schaer guides teachers and students in the process of making their own books by using a variety of styles and employing folded book forms, which challenge kids' notion of what a "book" can be.

- Grade levels: K-12

- $

Karen Lee Schmidt

361 West 22nd Street
New York, NY 10011
(212) 675-3086 phone/fax
karenleeschmidt@earthlink.net
<www.karenleeschmidt.net>

 As an illustrator of more than 30 children's books and an author of two, Karen Schmidt combines fun, humorous slides, and props to show students how a picture book is built, from start to finish. She gives students a "tour" of her studio and shares with them the secrets of where ideas come from and how those ideas turn into finished books.

- Grade levels: K-6

- $$

- *What Do You Love?* By Jonathan London, Harcourt, 2000, ISBN 0152019197

  The Jungle Baseball Game. By Tom Paxton, Morrow Junior Books, 1999, ISBN 0688067425

  You Be Good, I'll Be Night. By Eve Merriam, Morrow Junior Books, 1988, ISBN 0688067425

- Requirements: Slide projector, easel, sound system

Barbara Seuling

320 Central Park West, Apt. 6-I
New York, NY 10025
(212) 877-4457 phone/fax
aplbrk@aol.com

Barbara Seuling's favorite topics to discuss with children are how to write articles or stories, how a book is created, and the fun of researching "freaky fact" books. She also offers presentations on how to write a children's book and get it published.

- Grade levels: K-12

- $$$

- *Spring Song.* Gulliver Books, 2001, ISBN 0152023178

  Winter Lullaby. Brown Deer Press, 1998, ISBN 0152014039

How to Write a Children's Book and Get It Published. John Wiley & Sons, 1991, ISBN 0684103434

Phyllis Shalant

17 Palisade Avenue
White Plains, NY 10607
(914) 592-2278
nonshalant@aol.com
<www.shalant.com>

Phyllis Shalant's workshop on *Writing Like a Turtle* blends science with writing, getting kids to think "outside the bowl" and taking them into weirder and weirder drafts.

- Grade levels: 3-6
- $$

- *Bartleby of the Mighty Mississippi.* Dutton, 2000, ISBN 0525460330, New York Public Library Best Books

  The Great Eye. Puffin Books, 1996, ISBN 0141300728, Sunshine State Young Readers Master List

  Beware of Kissing Lizard Lips. Dutton, 1995, ISBN 0140384227, Texas Bluebonnet Master List

Robert Kimmel Smith

42 West 13th Street, 3-D
New York, NY 10011
(212) 807-9847
robtksmith@aol.com

Robert Kimmel Smith shares with students his long, funny, difficult struggle to become a writer (at 40) and how his love of books shaped his life. He tells the "stories behind the stories" of his long-time best-selling titles and encourages kids to read. He also shares tips with kids who like to write.

- Grade levels: 3-6
- $$$

- *Mostly Michael.* Dell, 1988, ISBN 044040097x

  Jelly Belly. Dell, 1982, ISBN 0440442079

  Chocolate Fever. Dell, 1978, ISBN 0440413699

Chris Soentpiet

2912A 164th Street
Flushing, NY 11358-1428
(718) 461-8889 phone/fax
chris@soentpiet.com
<www.soentpiet.com>

How do you get children excited about reading? Chris Soentpiet knows. His entertaining slide show and drawing demonstrations show kids how he puts together his multicultural books, from concept to completion.

- Grade levels: K-12
- $$$

- *Molly Bannaky.* By Alice McGill, Houghton Mifflin, 2000, ISBN 039572287x, Jane Addams Book Award, International Reading Association Children's Book of the Year, IRA Teacher's Choice 2000

  More Than Anything Else. By Marie Bradby, Scholastic/Orchard, 1995, ISBN 053-094642, IRA Book of the Year, IRA Teacher's Choice, American Library Association Notable Book, Notable Books for a Global Society Award, *Chicago Tribune* Top Ten, American Booksellers Association Pick of the List, *School Library Journal* starred review

- Requirements: Slide projector, microphone, large drawing pad, easel

Michele Sobel Spirn

514 10th Street
Brooklyn, NY 11215
(718) 499-7448
michelesteve21@hotmail.com

Thinking Like a Know-Nothing, Michele Spirn's program, introduces young students to four foolish friends who have many silly adventures and encourages kids to brainstorm even more adventures for these noodleheads. For older students, Michele talks about the key elements in writing a mystery and helps them formulate a hero, a villain, a crime, a motive, and a solution, with groups as large as 200.

- Grade levels: 1-8
- $$$

The Know-Nothings Talk Turkey. HarperCollins, 2000, ISBN 0060281847

The Bridges in London. Four Corners Publishing, 2000, ISBN 1893577007

The Know-Nothings. HarperCollins, 1995, ISBN 00644-2268

■ Requirements: Chalkboard, microphone

Javaka Steptoe

PO Box 330-170
Brooklyn, NY 11233-0170
(718) 363-2361 fax
javakas@yahoo.com
<www.javaka.com>
<www.javakasteptoe.com>

 Javaka Steptoe uses a slide presentation to introduce herself to youngsters and to kick off her "found art" workshops. She also offers haiku poetry workshops.

■ Grade levels: K-12

■ $$

■ *A Pocketful of Poems.* Clarion, 2001, ISBN 0395938686

Do You Know What I'll Do. HarperCollins, 2000, ISBN 006027879x

In Daddy's Arms I Am Tall. 1997, ISBN 1880000318, Coretta Scott King Award for illustration, NAACP Image Award nominee, Texas Bluebonnet Award

Catherine Stock

17 East 96th Street
New York, NY 10128
(212) 534-8941 phone/fax
StockScattyCat@cs.com
<www.catherinestock.com>

 Catherine Stock describes herself as an artist, an author, an illustrator, a designer, an art director, and a vagabond who loves to share her worldwide adventures with students. Kids enjoy hearing about the time she had to chase monkeys out of her tent in Malawi and the time she awoke covered with *savudi* (African army ants) in Tanzania. Catherine shows slides while recounting her adventures in Trinidad, Greece, France, Tanzania, South Africa, Zimbabwe, Mexico, and Malawi.

■ Grade levels: K-12

■ $$

■ *Gugu's House.* Clarion, 2001, ISBN 0618003894

Where Are You Going, Manyoni? Morrow Junior Books, 1993, ISBN 0688103529

Galimoto. By Karen Lynn Williams, Lothrop, Lee & Shepard, 1990, ISBN 0688087892

■ Requirements: Slide projector

George Sullivan

330 East 33rd Street, 7J
New York, NY 10016
(212) 689-9745
(212) 683-8064 fax
gjsbooks@aol.com

 George Sullivan is the author of more than 100 books for children and young adults. Most of his books are richly illustrated with photographs that he selected. In his school presentation, George uses original images from recent books to explain to kids the qualities that make a photograph dramatic and meaningful and gives students tips on improving their own pictures. He stresses that photography is a fairly recent invention and shows examples of daguerreotypes from the 1840s, card photographs from the 1860s (which were avidly collected by adults), and stereo cards from the 1880s.

■ Grade levels: 4-8

■ $$

■ *The Battle of Wounded Knee.* Scholastic, forthcoming

One Hundred Years in Photographs. Scholastic, 2000, ISBN 0590228587

Portraits of War: Civil War Photographers and Their Work. Twenty-first Century/Holt, 1998, ISBN 0761330194

Sam Swope

10 West 90th Street
New York, NY 10024
(212) 873-2720 phone/fax
samswope@aol.com

Like Sam Swope's books, his presentations mix fun and seriousness to show kids (via slides and music) the journey his ideas take from birth as napkin doodles to stories. He describes their many drafts, his search for publishers, and their appearance as books, as well as their subsequent misadventures in Hollywood, on the stage, and in the opera house. His writing workshops are based on years of teaching creative writing to all ages and utilize art, music, and acting to encourage even reluctant students to write poetry and prose.

- Grade levels: K-5
- $$

- *Jack and the Seven Deadly Giants.* Farrar, Straus & Giroux, forthcoming

  Gotta Go! Gotta Go! Farrar, Straus & Giroux, 2000, ISBN 0374327572, Nick Junior best book of the year

  Araboolies of Liberty Street. Farrar, Straus & Giroux, 1989, ISBN 0374303908, Parents' Choice Silver Honor, Maryland Black-Eyed Susan Award, adapted into a stage musical and opera

- Requirements: Slide projector, CD player, chalkboard

Linda Tagliaferro

248-44 Thebes Avenue
Little Neck, NY 11362-1252
(718) 423-0924
Linda5997@aol.com

Linda Tagliaferro offers easy-to-understand workshops on topics such as genetic engineering, cloning, engineered foods, and stem cells. She also shares her slides of the Galapagos Islands and the Pacific archipelago, the islands called the "living laboratory of evolution."

- Grade levels: K-12
- $-$$

- *Polar Bears.* NorthWord Press, forthcoming

  Galapagos Islands: Nature's Delicate Balance at Risk. Lerner, 2001, ISBN 0822506483, National Science Teachers Association/Children's Book Council Outstanding Science Trade Book 2002, Society of School Librarians International Book Awards Honor Book

  Genetic Engineering: Progress or Peril? Lerner, 1997, ISBN 0822526107, Bank Street College of Education Best Children's Books of the Year selection

- Requirements: Slide projector, TV/VCR, sound system for large groups

Erika Tamar

399 East 72nd Street, Apt. 16D
New York, NY 10021-4651
(212) 879-3843
erikatamar@earthlink.net

In her presentation, *Life Story of a Book*, Erika Tamar discusses her writing process with students, from the germ of an idea to publication. She also offers a workshop called *Strictly Personal,* in which she reveals how her own experience is used and disguised in fiction, then encourages children to use writing as a safe way to express joy, anger, and sorrow. Her fiction writing workshop for middle and high school uses unusual writing exercises to teach plotting, characterization, dialogue, setting, and how to use sense memory to evoke emotion. Erika has 19 books published and has won numerous awards from the American Library Association, the International Reading Association, and various states' lists.

- Grade levels: 4-12
- $$

- *The Midnight Train Home.* Dell, 2002, ISBN 0375901590, Western Writers of America Spur Award

  Alphabet City Ballet. HarperTrophy, 1997, ISBN 0064406687, Child Study's Children's Books of the Year, Junior Library Guild selection

  The Junkyard Dog. Knopf, 1995, ISBN 0679870571, 0439106192 pbk, California Young Readers Medal, Virginia Young Readers Award, published in Germany, Sweden, and France

Natasha A. Tarpley

133 West 112th Street, #5B
New York, NY 10026
(212) 865-6031
natarana@aol.com

Writing is an adventure fueled by pen and paper (or computer, if you prefer); a little imagination takes you father than anything on wheels or wings ever could. Natasha Tarpley speaks to young "travelers" and uses writing exercises derived from her book, *Girl in the Mirror*. She also offers a presentation on how to become a writer, which covers the process of book creation from inspiration to publishing contract.

- Grade levels: K-12

- $-$$$

- *What I Know Is Me: African American Teenage Girls on Life*. Doubleday, forthcoming

  Bippity Bop Barbershop! Little Brown, 2001, ISBN 0316522848

  I Love My Hair! Little Brown, 1998, ISBN 0316522759, Blackboard Children's Book of the Year Award 1999, Black Caucus American Library Association Top Recommended Book

- Requirements: Overhead projector, sound system

Timothy Tocher

c/o Meadowbrook Press
(800) 338-2232
To2im@aol.com
<www.FictionTeachers.com>

Tim Tocher is a retired teacher living in the Hudson River Valley whose school presentations include interactive poetry, in which students read and write humorous verse; classroom theater; and a program in which kids enjoy a slide show comparing their lives to those of kids in the 1950s.

- Grade levels: K-8

- $

- *Long Shot*. Meadowbrook Press, 2001, ISBN 06898433313

David Vanadia

206 East 17th Street
New York, NY 10003
(212) 539-1385 phone/fax
david@vswebs.com
<www.vswebs.com>

David Vanadia accompanies himself on bass guitar while telling his very original stories, which encourage listeners to combine stories with family history, folklore, and technology. David also gives a workshop on storytelling and the computer.

- Grade levels: 6-12

- $

- *Six Stories Tall*. CD, self-published, no ISBN

Vivian Vande Velde

VvandeVeld@aol.com

Vivian Vande Velde writes short stories, science fiction, and fantasy for readers of all ages. Her informal, anecdotal school talks describe how she began writing and show some of the stages a manuscript goes through during the publication process. She also answers questions such as, Where do you get your ideas? Who's in charge of illustrations? Are you rich? and Do you know J. K. Rowling/Stephen King?

- Grade levels: 4-12

- $$$

- *Troll Teacher*. Holiday House, 2000, ISBN 082341503

  Never Trust a Dead Man. Harcourt, 1999, ISBN 0152018999, Edgar Award 2000

  Smart Dog. Harcourt, 1998, ISBN 0152018476

- Requirements: Overhead projector

Marcella Bakur Weiner

383 Ocean Parkway
Brooklyn, NY 11218-4701
(718) 941-0318
(718) 856-5795 fax

 Dr. Marcella Weiner reads her book and guides her audience through the adventures of Toodles, who learns that though she began the story not loving herself, everybody is lovable.

- Grade levels: K-12
- $
- *A Woman's Voice: Stories of Biblical Women.* Jason Aronson, 2001, ISBN 0765761491

  I Want Your Moo: A Story for Children About Self-Esteem. Magination Press/American Psychological Association, 1996, ISBN 0945354657

Carol Weston

670 West End Avenue, 2F
New York, NY 10025
(212) 724-1311
carolwords@aol.com
<carolweston.com>
<melaniemartin.com>

Carol Weston comes to school with a bag of tricks. Not only does she show students her books, but she also shows their Chinese and Italian translations, early book jackets (complete with mistakes), and rejection letters. Carol also reads from her own third-grade diary and encourages students to keep journals. As the advice columnist for *Girls' Life Magazine*, she receives letters with questions, and she reads some of these, then asks students how *they* would respond.

- Grade levels: 2-9
- $
- *Melanie Martin Goes Dutch.* Knopf, 2002, ISBN 0375821953

  The Diary of Melanie Martin. Knopf, 2000, ISBN 0440416671

  Girltalk: All the Stuff Your Sister Never Told You. HarperCollins, 1985, ISBN 0060928506, New York Public Library Best Books for the Teen Age

Elizabeth Winthrop

250 West 90th Street, 6A
New York, NY 10024
(212) 721-5289 fax
Winthrop@absolute-sway.com
<www.absolute-sway.com/Winthrop>

Elizabeth Winthrop talks with students about her creative process when writing for children and adults and gives a slide show that answers that eternal question, Where do you get your ideas? She also gives mini writing workshops for older students and talks for parents, teachers, and librarians. Elizabeth's the author of more than 50 books for children, including *Castle in the Attic*, which won the Dorothy Canfield Fisher Award.

- Grade levels: 1-6
- $$
- *Dumpy La Rue.* Henry Holt, 2001, ISBN 0805063854

  Dear President Roosevelt. Winslow Press, 2001, ISBN 189087619

  Promises. Clarion, 2000, ISBN 0395822726
- Requirements: slide projector, microphone

Diane Wolkstein

10 Patchin Place
New York, NY 10011
(212) 929-6871 phone/fax
<www.dianewolkstein.com>

Whether recounting trickster stories, epics, or fairy tales, Diane Wolkstein speaks from the heart of each story she tells. Known for her meticulous research and her great range as a performer, she's also the author of more than 20 books of folklore.

- Grade levels: K-12
- $
- *The Magic Orange Tree.* Schocken, 1997, ISBN 0805210776

  Inanna, Queen of Heaven and Earth. HarperCollins, 1983, ISBN 0060908548

Jane Breskin Zalben

70 South Road
Port Washington, NY 11050
(516) 944-8590
(516) 944-8607 fax
janezalben@hotmail.com
<www.janebreskinzalben.com>

 Jane Zalben, an author of more than 45 books, a teacher at the School of Visual Arts, and a former art director at Scribners, shows kids slide and materials that reveal how a picture book is made, from the first germ of an idea to the finished book. She also discusses how an author might get an idea for a chapter book.

- Grade levels: K-12
- $$$
- Requirements: Portable microphone, carousel slide projector, long table

Melanie Zimmer

Dancing Bear Puppet Theater
30 Van Epps Street
Vernon, NY 13476
(315) 829-4898 phone/fax
Melanie@dreamscape.com
<www.thepuppets.com>

Melanie Zimmer's shows include *The Littlest Pirate*, a fabulously funny hand-puppet show, and *Maiyarap's Magic Dust*, featuring Thai marionettes and the telling of Hindu myth (the Ramakien) through Thai classical dance. At the end of *Maiyarap's Magic Dust*, students learn the dance of Maiyarap the Giant. Melanie also offers walk-around puppetry and processional puppetry for fairs and festivals.

- Grade levels: K-12
- $

Joyce A. Zucker

PO Box 1152
East Northport, NY 11731
(631) 261-5104

Joyce Zucker isn't just a teacher and a professional musical storyteller—she's also a writer and an inventor of educational musical games and table games. Her *Make-It* columns have appeared in *Long Island Parent* for years.

- Grade levels: K-12
- $

North Carolina

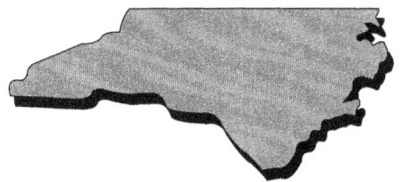

Frances A. Davis

104 Barnhill Place
Chapel Hill, NC 27514-9224
(919) 967-2549 or (919) 967-2452
(919) 967-6643 fax
eld513@earthlink.net

A slide show on the evolution of Frank Lloyd Wright's work is just one of the student presentation topics Frances Davis offers. She's also a regional advisor for the Society of Children's Book Writers and Illustrators and loves to talk to kids about the process of writing a nonfiction book.

- Grade levels: K-8
- $
- *Frank Lloyd Wright: Maverick Architect.* Lerner, 1996, ISBN 0822549530
- Requirements: Slide projector

Ron I. Jones

2305 Englewood Avenue
Durham, NC 27705
(919) 286-7995
ron@rijones.com
<www.rijones.com>

Ron Jones has more than 25 years' experience telling stories at schools, libraries, festivals, and museums. He offers traditional folklore, classic, and contemporary stories, including participatory tales and songs on his guitar. Ron also offers storytelling residencies and consulting on storytelling festivals.

- Grade levels: K-12
- $$

MariJo Moore

PO Box 2493
Candler, NC 28715-9236
(828) 665-7630
(828) 670-6347 fax
marijom@aol.com
<www.marijomoore.com>

MariJo Moore's objective when speaking to young people is to reveal writing as a spiritual exercise that leads us to a deeper understanding of our connection to the whole.

- Grade levels: 6-12
- $$$$
- *Red Woman with Backward Eyes and Other Stories.* Renegade Planets Publishing, 2001, ISBN 0965492176

  The Cherokee Little People. Rigby, 2000, ISBN 0763566632

  Feeding the Ancient Fires: A Collection of Writings by North Carolina American Indians. Crossroads, 1999, ISBN 0967218004

Connie Regan-Blake

PO Box 2898
Asheville, NC 28802
(828) 258-1113
(828) 253-2956 fax
storyplace@charter.net
<www.storywindow.com>

Drawing on her Irish heritage, Southern roots, and sense of humor, Connie Regan-Blake's talent turns a packed theater into an intimate circle of friends. One of the first to bring storytelling to a national audience, as part of the Folktellers duo and as a solo performance artist, she helped shape and ignite the storytelling revival that occurred more than 25 years ago. Her audio and video recordings are available from Mythic Stream, at the above address.

- Grade levels: K-12

- $$

- Requirements: Microphone

Wayne and Jane Sims

Lynx Drive
Black Mountain, NC 28711-9774
(828) 664-1429
storybuff@aol.com
<www.schoolshows.com>

Tandem tellers, offering folktales, humor, historical pieces, legends, and literary pieces, as well as a segment called *True or Ought To Be*, the "Storytelling Sims" offer a great listening experience for audiences.

- Grade levels: K-12

- $

Michael "Badhair" Williams

Route 1 Box 304
Zirconia, NC 28790
(828) 693-1702
(828) 692-0091 fax
badhair@a-o.com

When was the last time you saw a giant walk through your back yard? Have you seen a ghost in the attic? Have you ever seen a man ride a lion through the middle of town in front of the King? Well if it's been awhile, you haven't heard Michael Badhair Williams telling tales.

- Grade levels: K-12 (PG-10 for scarier shows)

- $$

Ohio

Elizabeth Alder

4558 River Street
Willoughby, OH 44094
(440) 942-1187
(440) 975-4301 fax
Alder1066@aol.com

Elizabeth Alder makes history sizzle with presentations such as *Normans-1, Anglo-Saxons-0,* and *But It Was Theirs First,* about the War of 1812 from the viewpoint of an Irish/Mohawk translator and warrior. She also offers writing workshops on crafting historical fiction.

- Grade levels: 6-9
- $$$
- *Crossing the Panther's Path.* Farrar, Straus & Giroux, 2002, ISBN 0374316627

  The King's Shadow. Farrar, Straus & Giroux, 1995, ISBN 0374341826, American Library Association Best Book for YA, International Reading Association Children's Book Award, *School Library Journal* Best Book of the Year, Friends of American Writers Award

Liz Ball

PO Box 63
Tipp City, OH 45371
(937) 667-6288
(937) 669-4178 fax
HiddenPictures@aol.com
<members.aol.com/Hiddenpictures>

With her puzzle apron, posters, and entertaining sketches, Liz Ball sets the mood for hidden-picture puzzle fun as she encourages her audiences' creativity by involving them in her "how to draw" demo.

- Grade levels: K-6
- $$
- *ABC—What Job Do You See?* Hidden Pictures, 2002, ISBN 0967815924

  Holiday Hidden Treasures. Hidden Pictures, 2000, ISBN 0967815916

  Hidden Treasures. Hidden Pictures, 1999, ISBN 0967815908

- Requirements: Easel

Rick Carson

1070 Azel Avenue
Hamilton, OH 45013
(513) 867-1525
jrcarson@fuse.net

Rick Carson brings an unusual blend of dramatic skills and traditional concepts to the art of storytelling, whether he's encouraging school children to read, swapping true stories with others, or reviving a traditional form of entertainment. He's been a featured teller at the Corn Island Festival and the National Storytelling Conference.

- Grade levels: K-12
- $

Giggles and Ghosts. Cassette, self-published, no ISBN

How I Learned to Cuss and Other Stories You Shouldn't Hear. Cassette, self-published, no ISBN

Brian P. Cleary

16505 Southland Avenue
Cleveland, OH 44111
(216) 889-1799
(216) 889-1789 fax
BabeRuth60@aol.com
<www.briancleary.com>

Brian Cleary does stand-up comedy about his rise from being an odd, quirky kid with a short attention span to being an odd, quirky adult with a short attention span. He reads books, teaches wordplay, and engages kids in anagrams and palindromes—all the while leading them to write poetry.

- Grade levels: K-12
- $$

Hairy Scary Ordinary, What Is an Adjective? Carolrhoda, 2001, ISBN 1575054027

A Mink a Fink a Skating Rink, What Is a Noun? Carolrhoda, 2000, ISBN 1575054019

Jamaica Sandwich? Carolrhoda, 1996, 0822521148

Dandi Daley Mackall

1254 Tupelo Lane
West Salem, OH 44287
dmackall@ashland.edu
<www.dandibooks.com>

Dandi Mackall's program includes an all-student assembly that weaves writing and reading information into stories—true, funny stories of things that happened to her when she was the kids' age. She also offers a workshop on the silent-movie era (ties in with her picture book, *Silent Dreams*). Dandi's the author of 12 series and more than 250 books.

- Grade levels: K-12
- $$

Are We There Yet, Mom? Dutton/Doubleday, forthcoming

Whinny the Horse Whisperer series. Tyndale Publishing, 6 books, forthcoming

Off to Bethlehem. HarperCollins, 2002, ISBN 069415059

Brandon Marie Miller

6959 Rosemary Lane
Cincinnati, OH 45236
(513) 984-3544
PBJ2@worldnet.att.net

Brandon Marie Miller offers workshops on writing, using active words, our senses, and the mind's eye, as well as a session on writing nonfiction using research, organization, writing, and revision skills. She also offers history presentations on a variety of topics, such as *Growing Up in Colonial America*, *Women of the Old West*, *History of Fashion*, and *History of Medicine—from Leeches to Lasers*. All of her talks include visuals and props.

- Grade levels: K-8
- $$

Dressed for the Occasion: What Americans Wore, 1620-1970. Lerner, 1999, ISBN 0822517388, Children's Book Committee of Bank Street College Best Children's Books of 2000

Just What the Doctor Ordered; The History of American Medicine. Lerner, 1997, ISBN 082251737x, International Reading Association Children's Book Award, Society of Midland Authors

Buffalo Gals: Women of the Old West. Lerner, 1995, ISBN 0822517302, National Council for Social Studies Notable Book, IRA Teachers' Choice, Society of School Librarians International Outstanding Book

- Requirements: Overhead projector, table, sound system, dry-erase board, slide projector

Candace R. Miller

439 South Cole Street
Lima, OH 45805
(419) 227-2516
bode@wcoil.com

Candace Miller performs nature legends from around the world, how-and-why stories about the naming, creation, and characteristics of plants and animals. In addition to her *Young Author* workshops, in which she leads students in writing their own nature legends, she also gives professional development workshops on storytelling for the shy and intimidated. She's been named the foremost plant storyteller in the world by Dr. Marc Cathey, President Emeritus of the American Horticultural Society.

- Grade levels: K-12
- $

- *Tales from the Creature Kingdom.* Pourquoi Press, 1997, self-published, no ISBN

  Tales from the Bird Kingdom. Pourquoi Press, 1996, self-published, no ISBN

  Tales from the Plant Kingdom. Pourquoi Press, 1995, self-published, no ISBN

- Requirements: Small table, chair

Bonnie Pryor

19600 Baker Road
Gambier, OH 43022
(740) 427-2427
(740) 397-8481 fax
chrissy@ecr.net

Bonnie Pryor uses family stories to explain writing concepts to students and to show them how ideas for books can develop from everyday life. She describes her childhood, which was filled with books and the love of reading—so she says it was almost inevitable for her to become a writer. She also explains to kids the process of how an idea becomes a book, in hopes that they, too, will learn to love books and reading. Bonnie's won the Irma Simonton Black Award, has been nominated for an Edgar Award, and is on a variety of outstanding book lists.

- Grade levels: K-6
- $$

- *Joseph's Choice: 1861.* Avon, 2002, ISBN 0380733218

  Grandpa Bear's Christmas. Illustrated by Bruce Degen, Mulberry Books, 1999, ISBN 0688170668

  Vinegar Pancakes and Vanishing Cream. Beech Tree, 1996, ISBN 0688147445

Jan Wahl

6766 Carrietowne Lane
Toledo, OH 43617
(419) 841-5624

Jan Wahl solicits story or poem material from students (with some advance preparation) and plays editor, awarding prizes when he arrives at a school. Jan also reads stories and shows slides or videos of his books. He's won the Hopwood Prize, the Ohioana Award, the Christopher Medal, the Redbook Award, the *Parents Magazine* Award, and the Young Critics Prize from the Bologna Book Fair, among others.

- Grade levels: K-6
- $$

- *Pleasant Fieldmouse.* Illustrated by Maurice Sendak, HarperCollins, 2003 reissue, ISBN 0060297263

  I Met a Dinosaur. Illustrated by Chris Sheban, The Creative Company, 2002, ISBN 0898123313 pbk

  Elf Night. Illustrated by Peter Weevers, Carolrhoda, 2002, ISBN 1575055120

Pennsylvania

Barbara Baumgartner

455 West Harvey Street
Philadelphia, PA 19144-3818
(215) 849-3818
barbara909@yahoo.com
<www.BarbaraStories.com>

Barbara Baumgartner tells captivating folk tales from many cultures, leads audiences in sonorous chants, and performs retellings using stick puppets.

- Grade levels: K-6
- $$
- *All My Shining Silver: Stories of Value from Around the World.* Dorling Kindersley, 2000, ISBN 0789466635

    Good as Gold: Stories of Values from Around the World. Dorling Kindersley, 1998, ISBN 0789434822

    Crocodile! Crocodile! Stories Told Around the World. Dorling Kindersley, 1994, ISBN 1564584631

Jane Buchanan

258 Jefferson Street
Meadville, PA 16335
(814) 336-3770
writeme@janebuchanan.com
<www.janebuchanan.com>

 Jane Buchanan shares a short slide show about herself and her books, then talks about the process of writing and her experiences with dyslexia. She offers presentations on writing historical fiction, the Orphan Train movement, writing from real life, and the use of research tools and techniques. She loves to answer questions about her books (including why she did that to the cat in *Gratefully Yours*).

- Grade levels: 3-12
- $$
- *The Berry-Picking Man.* Farrar, Straus & Giroux, 2003, ISBN 0374406103

    Hank's Story. Farrar, Straus & Giroux, 2001, ISBN 0374328366

    Gratefully Yours. Farrar, Straus & Giroux, 1997, ISBN 0374327750, Georgia Children's Book Award nominee, Mark Twain Award, Golden Sower Award, Great Stone Face Award, Sequoyah Book Award, Volunteer State Book Award, Sunshine State Young Reader Award

- Requirements: Slide projector, overhead projector

Shari Faden Donahue

PO Box 53
Washington Crossing, PA 18977
(215) 862-5899
(215) 862-7055 fax
Arimax1@aol.com
<www.Arimaxkids.com>

 Shari Donahue's presentation on how to publish books includes a PowerPoint presentation of how the dimensional collages in *Zebra-Striped Whale* were created and

gives students the opportunity to create a similar piece of art. She also discusses following one's dreams, which is the book's theme.

- Grade levels: K-6
- $$-$$$
- *The Zebra-Striped Whale with the Polka-Dot Tail.* Arimax, 2001, ISBN 096342873

  Celebrate Hanukkah with Me. Arimax, 1998, ISBN 096342872

  My Favorite Family Haggadah. Arimax, 1994, ISBN 0963428713

Judith Gorog

1275 Wheatland Avenue
Lancaster, PA 17603
(717) 293-8113
jagged@epix.net

Judith Gorog connects with audiences—teachers have even been known to stop grading papers in the back of the room, because they've become fully engaged in Judith's program. "Please tell one more," audiences ask. Judith weaves stories through discussions of idea sources, writing structure, editing, and publishing in presentations filled with humor and challenging ideas. Teachers use her stories for units on the short story and the urban legend, and their relation to folk and cautionary tales.

- Grade levels: K-12
- $$$
- *When Nobody's Home,* Scholastic, 1996, ISBN 059046874X

Linda Oatman High

1209 Reading Road
Narvon, PA 17555
(717) 445-8246 phone/fax
lohigh@desupernet.net
<www.lindaoatmanhigh.com>

Linda Oatman High's school visits sizzle with fun and creativity as she presents her slide show, *Writing to the Beat of a Different Drummer,* which is followed by writing games and exercises. Linda's the author of many children's books, as well as short stories, stage plays, and screenplays, and travel, feature, and fiction articles for magazines and newspapers.

- Grade levels: K-8
- $$
- *A Humble Life: Plain Poems.* Illustrated by Bill Farnsworth, Eerdmans, 2001, ISBN 0802852076

  Under New York. Holiday House, 2001, ISBN 0823415511

  Barn Savers. Boyds Mills, 1999, ISBN 1563974037
- Requirements: Slide projector, microphone

Elizabeth Fitzgerald Howard

825 Morewood Avenue
Pittsburgh, PA 15213
(412) 605-0293

Elizabeth Fitzgerald Howard's books are based on incidents from the lives of people in her family, including Aunt Flossie's hat flying into the water, cousin Chita's remembrances of her papa's wild Spanish-American War adventures, and Great Aunt Virgie and her brothers walking seven miles to their Quaker school. Elizabeth brings these tales to life in her presentations through dramatic storytelling and the judicious use of sepia slides of the actual people.

- Grade levels: K-6
- $$
- *Lulu's Birthday.* Greenwillow, 2001, ISBN 0688159443, Parents' Choice Silver Honor

  Aunt Flossie's Hats (and Crabcakes Later). Clarion, 2001, ISBN 0618120386

  Virgie Goes to School with Us Boys. Simon & Schuster, 2000, ISBN 0689800762, Pennsylvania Library Association Carolyn Field Award, Coretta Scott King Award
- Requirements: Slide projector, microphone, prefers library venue

Sally Keehn

1691 Lehigh Parkway North
Allentown, PA 18103
(610) 770-0274
sallykeehn@aol.com
<author-illustr-source.com/sallykeehn.htm>

From Battlefields to Gravestones: The Search for Story is Sally Keehn's topic on the writing process and how students can tap into the process by exploring the world inside and outside themselves. She uses a slide show, historical artifacts, and a game to reveal the journey an author takes to bring the past alive for young readers.

- Grade levels: 4-12
- $$

- *Anna Sunday.* Philomel, 2002, ISBN 0399238751

  Moon of Two Dark Horses. Philomel, 1995, ISBN 039-227830, 0440412870 pbk, New York Public Library Best Books List, Bank Street Children's Book of the Year

  I Am Regina. Philomel, 1991, ISBN 0399217975, 0440407540 pbk, Pennsylvania Library Association Carolyn W. Field Award, Jefferson Cup Honor Book, National Council for Social Studies Notable Book, International Reading Association Young Adult's Choice, New York Public Library Books for the Teen Age

- Requirements: Carousel slide projector, screen, microphone, table

Judy Lalli

601 Monroe Drive
Harleysville, PA 19438-3916
judele@aol.com

Judy Lalli discusses her experiences as an author during her school visits. She leads small- and large-group presentations on the social skills featured in her books: believing in yourself, learning from mistakes, sharing, cooperating, peacemaking, and celebrating diversity. She also conducts workshops on poetry writing.

- Grade levels: K-5
- $

- *I Like Being Me: Poems for Children About Feeling Special, Appreciating Others and Getting Along.* Free Spirit, 1997, ISBN 1575420252, Early Childhood News Directors' Choice Award

  Make Someone Smile and 40 More Ways to Be a Peaceful Person. Free Spirit, 1996, ISBN 0815793997, American Booksellers Association Pick of the Lists

- Requirements: Overhead projector

Kathy Long

43 Third Avenue
Lehighton, PA 18235
(610) 377-0428
kalstory@ptd.net

Kathy Long inspires and motivates students with storytelling sessions that include audience participation, sign language, and her "anti-bully" program, which combines folktales with personal stories.

- Grade levels: K-12
- $

- *Taylor Twinkle Finds a Home.* Best Friends Press, 1994, ISBN 0964206307

  Living in Harmony. Best Friends Press, 1995, ISBN 0964206315

David Lubar

4695 Oakwood Lane
Nazareth, PA 18064
dlubar@aol.com
<www.davidlubar.com>

David Lubar's presentation answers the one big question, "Where do you get your ideas?" by using techniques that lead students to try their own hand at writing. His interactive, energetic workshop includes readings and sharing stories about the writing life, as well as tales of his "secret" life as a video-game programmer and designer with credits including *Home Alone* and *Frogger2*.

- Grade levels: 4-8
- $$

Dunk. Clarion, 2002, ISBN 061819455x

Hidden Talents. Tor, 1999, ISBN 0812541707, American Library Association Best Books for Young Adults

Monster Road. Scholastic, 1999, ISBN 0590281682

- Requirements: Overhead projector

Robin Moore

Box 181
Springhouse, PA 19477
(215) 646-2150
robin@comcat.com
<www.robin-moore.com>

Robin Moore isn't just a storyteller (although he tells traditional and original stories and accompanies himself on the flute, hunting horn, and Celtic harp)—he's a performance artist and an author of many titles on sustaining the writing process and encouraging family storytelling. Robin's programs often include demonstrations of old-time living skills and nature lore.

- Grade levels: K-12
- $$

The Man with the Silver Oar. HarperCollins, 2002, ISBN 0060000481

The Natural Born Writer. Sounds True, 2001, ISBN 1564558495

Creating a Family Storytelling Tradition. August House, 1999, ISBN 0874835658

Rebecca O'Connell

272 46th Street
Pittsburgh, PA 15201
(412) 683-8796
<www.frontstreetbooks.com>

Read Widely, Write Well is Rebecca O'Connell's description of her path to publication. Her funny, lively presentation of the same name includes online and print resources helpful to writers. She also answers questions such as, Where can writers get ideas? How do they prepare a manuscript? and How and where do they submit their work?

- Grade levels: 7-12
- $

Myrtle of Willendorf. Front Street Books, 2000, ISBN 1886910529, New York Public Library Books for the Teen Age

Susan Shaw

437 Sharon Drive
Wayne, PA 19087
(610) 971-9378
sues437@juno.com

Susan Shaw's school presentation helps students knock down walls that limit their creative endeavors using humor and examples to help them turn ideas into stories.

- Grade levels: K-12
- $

Black-Eyed Suzie. Boyds Mills, 2002, ISBN 156397729x

Nancy Springer

417 Lake Meade Drive
East Berlin, PA 17316
(717) 259-0257
nancyspringer@blazenet.net

Nancy Springer's *Seven Serious Questions* workshop inspires students to brainstorm and begin writing their own works of fiction. This hands-on story-starter galvanizes reluctant writers and enthusiastic young authors. Nancy also motivates active reading with her *Black Marks on White Paper* seminar, which gives unusual insights into the co-creative partnership between fiction writer and reader. She's won the Mystery Writers Edgar Allen Poe Award twice, as well as the Pennsylvania School Librarians Outstanding Pennsylvania Author Award.

- Grade levels: 3-12
- $$

Rowan Hood: Outlaw Girl of Sherwood Forest. Philomel, 2001, ISBN 0399233687

Separate Sisters. Holiday House, 2001, ISBN 0823415449

I Am Mordred: A Tale of Camelot. Philomel, 1998, ISBN 0399231439, 0698118413 pbk,

Publishers Weekly star forecast, *Booklist* Top Ten Fantasy, Carolyn W. Field Award, American Library Association Best Books for Young Adults

Ellen Norman Stern

135 Anbury Lane
Willow Grove, PA 19090
(215) 657-2372
estern@erols.com

Ellen Stern loves to write and speak about heroes who've unraveled history and applied its lessons to the present, as well as people who've helped to overcome injustices and others who've tried to make the world a better place.

- Grade levels: 10-12
- $
- *The French Physician's Boy: A Story of Philadelphia's 1793 Yellow Fever Epidemic.* Xlibris, 2001, ISBN 0738858765, 0738858773 pbk
- *Elie Wiesel: A Voice for Humanity.* Jewish Publication Society, 1996, ISBN 08027605749, 0827605748 pbk

Ed Stivender

c/o Clancy Agency
5138 Whitehall Drive
Clifton Heights, PA 19018
(610) 259-8825
storyclan@aol.com

Since 1975, Ed Stivender has toured North America, Ireland, Indonesia, New Zealand, and Canada with his one-man shows that combine humor, music, song, story, and sometimes seriousness. He's "fabulated" at all of the major storytelling festivals (and all over the world) and has been received into the National Storytelling Association's Circle of Excellence. Ed's a Shakespearean actor, a banjo player, a teacher, a theologian, a Mummer, a dreamer, a juggler, and a raconteur, as well as an ex-teacher.

- Grade levels: K-12
- $$-$$$
- *Tellin' Time.* Klarity Multimedia, 2001, CD, ISBN 6065483192
- *Still Catholic After All These Fears.* August House, 1995, ISBN 0874834031
- *Raised Catholic, Can You Tell?* August House, 1992, ISBN 0874833361
- Requirements: Two microphones on stands

David Lorenz Winston

6655 McCallum Street, #408
Philadelphia, PA 19119
(215) 844-4675 phone/fax

David Winston is a fine-art and nature photographer who loves photographing animals. He also enjoys giving slide presentations about his *Life on the Farm* series, his photographic journeys, and various photography subjects. His work has been published by UNICEF, Hallmark, and the Wildlife Federation and has won many awards.

- Grade levels: 3-12
- $$
- *Life on a Farm* series. Carolrhoda, 2001 or 2002, various ISBNs, includes *Pigs, Goats, Horses, Cattle, Crop, Sheep, Chicken, Dairy,* and *Orchard* titles

Kay Winters

PO Box 339
Richlandtown, PA 18955
(215) 536-7355
(215) 536-4699 fax
KayWin@aol.com
<www.kaywinters.com>

As a former classroom teacher, a reading specialist, and a teacher of teachers, Kay Winters knows you can't talk *at* children—you have to talk *with* them. In her interactive assembly children form a poetry troupe and perform poems with faculty, staff, and audience, using choral speaking. Kay also uses slides to emphasize the importance of reading and to explain the process of writing.

- Grade levels: K-8
- $$

Did You See What I Saw? Poems About School. Viking, 2001, ISBN 01405266

Tiger Trail. Simon & Schuster, 2001, ISBN 0689823231

The Teeny Tiny Ghost. HarperCollins, 1997, ISBN 0064435903

Susan Wojciechowski

972 Somerset Lane
York, PA 17403
(717) 845-9647
swojciec@ycp.edu
<goose.ycp.edu/~swojciec>

In her school visits, Susan Wojciechowski talks about life, writing, and how books get published. She tries to get kids excited about reading and writing by presenting herself as an ordinary person who makes reading and writing a regular part of her life. Susan's earned the Christopher Medal, the Kate Greenaway Award, the American Library Association Notable Award, the International Reading Association Teacher's Choice, and the *New York Times* Editor's Choice.

- Grade levels: K-8
- $$
- *Beany Goes to Camp.* Candlewick, 2001, ISBN 076361615x

  The Best Halloween of All. Candlewick, 1998, ISBN 0763612413

  The Christmas Miracle of Jonathan Toomey. Candlewick, 1995, ISBN 1564023206

Judy Wolfman

2770 Hartford Road
York, PA 17402-3942
(717) 757-1953
(717) 840-8487 fax
jbwolfman@netrax.net

Judy Wolfman's an author and story teller who offers workshops called *Getting the Creative Juices Flowing* and *Start Writing NOW!*, as well as sessions on reading books effectively to kids and on the journey from idea to finished book. She's the author of plays, a musical, and a series of books, and has developed a series of reader's theater scripts.

- Grade levels: K-12
- $
- *Life on a (Pig/Goat/Cattle/Horse/Sheep/Dairy) Farm* series. Carolrhoda, various dates and ISBNs

  "Joseph the Tailor" and "A Hen or a Horse," Readers Theatre scripts. In Mel White's *Readers Theater Anthology*, Meriwether Publishing, 1992, ISBN 0916260860

  The Real Story of Little Red Riding Hood script. Pioneer Drama Service, no date, no ISBN

- Requirements: Carousel slide projector, table, flip chart, microphone

Susan Kimmel Wright

221 Fawcett Church Road
Bridgeville, PA 15017-1512
wereallwright@icubed.com

Susan Wright shares with kids the story of how she became a writer, how a bright idea became a story, and how her scribbled story became a book—complete with hands-on props. She also enjoys leading workshops with smaller groups and sharing the how-to's of writing good stories, creating good characters who live and breathe, and building exciting plots.

- Grade levels: 4-12
- $
- *Dead Letters.* Herald Press, 1996, ISBN 083619036x

  Death by Baby-sitting. Herald Press, 1994, ISBN 083613694x

  Secret of the Old Graveyard. Herald Press, 1993, ISBN 0836136276

Rhode Island

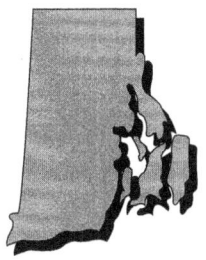

Linda Crotta Brennan

12 Teakwood Drive
Coventry, RI 02816
brennan@ids.net
<users.ids.net/~brennan/kidwrit.htm>

Linda Brennan offers a variety of work shops, such as *Sizzles and Fizzles* (the writer's life), *Stories to Go* (brainstorming a story), *Recipes for Iced Bugs and Slime* (writing nonfiction), and *Critique Without Tears* (for kids who have drafts of a story they can work on).

- Grade levels: K-12
- $
- *Bridge Over the Singing River.* Moon Mountain Publishing, forthcoming

  Marshmallow Kisses. Houghton Mifflin, 2000, ISBN 0395728725, Bank Street College Best Children's Books of the Year, Oppenheim Toy Portfolio Gold Award

  Flannel Kisses. Houghton Mifflin, 1997, ISBN 0395736811

Len Cabral

30 Marcy Street
Cranston, RI 02905
(401) 781-0019
(401) 781-0020 fax
Len@lencabral.com
<www.lencabral.com>

For more than 25 years, storyteller and author Len Cabral has been enchanting audiences with his African and Caribbean folktales, as well as original tales, personal stories of his Cape Verdean heritage, and tales from around the world. Len travels extensively throughout the U.S., building bridges across cultural boundaries through mime, poetry, song, humor, and characterization. He's been featured at the National Storytelling Festival, the Smithsonian Theater, and the Kennedy Center, and was recently honored with the Circle of Excellence Award by the National Storytelling Network.

- Grade levels: K-12
- $$
- *Len Cabral's Storytelling Book.* Neal Schuman Publishers, 1997, ISBN 1555702538

  Anansi's Narrow Waist. Addison Wesley, 1994, ISBN 0673362000, 0673362949 (Spanish)

Marc Joel Levitt

20 Pinehurst Street
Wakefield, RI 02879
(401) 783-0887
(401) 783-9064 fax
Marclevitt@aol.com

 Marc Levitt's program combines story telling, a literary memoir style, humor, and knowledge of folk traditions. His stories reflect his New York City childhood, his world travels, and his work experiences, including stints in the Merchant Marines, at lobster fishing, in radio production, and as a medicine show vaudevillian.

- Grade levels: K-12

- $$$
- *Johnny Appleseed Meets Paul Bunyan.* Pamet River Productions, forthcoming

  Johnny Appleseed. August House, 2001, ISBN 087431768

  Tales from an October Moon. August House, 1994, ISBN 0784832098

Barbara Keevil Parker

31 White Avenue
Riverside, RI 02915
(401) 433-4152 phone/fax
bkeevil5@aol.com

Barbara Parker's programs focus on nature and feature topics such as understanding wolves, learning about cheetahs, and getting to know giraffes. Her Earth Day presentations include a short play about frogs and hands-on activities. She also discusses with kids what it's like to be a writer and describes the journey of an idea from germination to finished book.

- Grade levels: K-6
- $
- *Giraffes: Gentle Giants.* Carolrhoda, 2003, ISBN pending

  North American Wolves. Carolrhoda, 1998, ISBN 1575050951

  Susan B. Anthony: Daring to Vote. Millbrook, 1998, ISBN 0761303585

Gayle Pearson

16 Marlborough Street
East Greenwich, RI 02818
(401) 884-7830
(401) 884-3033 fax
Gayle_Pearson@brown.edu

Gayle Pearson uses selections from her own work as jumping off points for discussions with students. She speaks with them about how good short stories can leave you breathless (and she knows they're a great way to teach students narrative form) and about where characters come from, how authors know what should happen next, and the most important thing about revising and rewriting.

- Grade levels: 5-8
- $
- *Don't Call It Paradise.* Simon & Schuster/Atheneum, 1999, ISBN 068982579x

  The Secret Box. Simon & Schuster/Atheneum, 1997, ISBN 068913791

Melodie L. C. Thompson

23 Anstis Street
Cranston, RI 02905
(401) 941-9838
sbmelody@yahoo.com

Melodie Thompson's storytelling roots go deep and wide, and her tale telling evokes laughter (*Enough Apples, How the Butterfly Tamed the Lion, Ants Don't Dance*) or touches the heart (*The Flea People, Pan y Agua, Different Drummer*). She also performs in the character of *Cathay Williams*, America's only female Buffalo Soldier, who fought in the Indian wars posing as a man.

- Grade levels: K-12
- $

Erin T. Whalen

PO Box 17382
Smithfield, RI 02917
(401) 233-9623 fax
<www.charlieshead.com>

 Erin Whalen explains to students each stage of how she created her children's books and shows them actual samples of the works for kids to hold and investigate. During Erin's presentation, students also have an opportunity to try her coloring techniques, using markers and colored pencils, just like in her illustrations. She uses her laptop to show kids how she turns finished text and illustrations into CDs that are shipped to her printer in Hong Kong.

- Grade levels: K-12
- $
- *Charlie's Head . . . a series.* Lily & Co., 1999, ISBN 1929265018 pbk

Naomi Flink Zucker

25 Locust Drive
Kingston, RI 02881
(401) 789-6175
NLZucker@uri.edu

If books are magic, then writers are magicians. But writers, like magicians, have to work long and hard to create illusions. In her school visits, Naomi Zucker shares the magic—and the secret of the magician behind the curtains—to encourage students to look closely at the craft before trying their own hand at it.

- Grade levels: 4-8

- $$

- *Joseph the Silent.* Dutton, forthcoming

  Benno's Bear. Dutton, 2001, ISBN 0525465219, Junior Library Guild selection, Smithsonian Notable Book, *Booklist* Editor's Choice

- Requirements: Overhead projector, screen

South Carolina

Gene Fehler

106 Laurel Lane
Seneca, SC 29678
(864) 882-8574
fehler@earthlink.net

Gene Fehler's poetry writing workshops, *From Idea to Poem* and *What to Do When a Poem Hits You,* share the fun of poetry, often through sports. Gene believes that every youngster is a potential poet and virtually all of them love poetry—once they've had the opportunity to discover what it sounds and looks like.

- Grade levels: 3-12
- $
- *Dancing on the Basepaths: Baseball Poetry and Verse.* McFarland & Co., 2001, ISBN 0786411023

  Tales from Baseball's Golden Age. Sports Publishing Inc., 2000, ISBN 1582612471

  Let the Poems Begin: A Poet's Guide to Writing Poetry. Good Apple, 2000, ISBN 0768203317

Suzette Hawkins

264 Crosson Street
Leesville, SC 29070
(803) 532-4592
shawkins@lex.lib.sc.us

Suzette Hawkins isn't only a children's library assistant—she's also studied under storytellers Augusta Baker and Laura Simms, and told tales with Jackie Torrence, David Holt, and Linda Goss. Suzette offers a wide variety of stories, and has organized the *So the Story Goes* events, which feature telling ghost tales in parks, for many years.

- Grade levels: K-12
- $

Dinah Johnson

6301 North Trenholm Road
Columbia, SC 29206
(803) 782-2097
(803) 777-9064 fax
Dianne@sc.edu
<www.sc.edu>

Dinah Johnson, a writer of picture books and a scholar of African-American children's literature, offers engaging, informative slide presentations and readings of her stories and poems.

- Grade levels: 6-12
- $$
- *Quinnie Blue.* Illustrated by James Ransome, Holt, 2000, ISBN 0805043780

  Sitting Pretty: A Celebration of Black Dolls. Photographs by Jules Pinkney, Holt, 2000, ISBN 0805060979

  All Around Town: The Photographs of Richard Samuel Roberts. Henry Holt, 1998, ISBN 0805054561

- Requirements: Slide projector

Sandy F. Richardson

19 Courtney court
Sumter, SC 29154
(903) 481-4811
phrichardson@infoave.net

Sandy Richardson offers several presentations: *Story Starts* uses visual examples from her works to provide kids with practical ideas on creating original stories. *Practicing the Process* uses hands-on writing exercises to jump-start students' creativity. *Writing Family Stories* explores interview techniques and carving a story from information. *Painting with Words* introduces kids to imagery and the power of verbs in writing.

- Grade levels: 5-12

- $

- *The Girl Who Ate Chicken Feet.* Dial, 1998, ISBN 0803722540, Bank Street College Best Books List

Lynn Floyd Wright

6317 Olde Knight Parkway
Columbia, SC 29209
(803) 647-1146
(803) 647-0197 fax
davelynn@ix.netcom.com

Lynn Floyd Wright takes students through the entire creative process from the author's point of view, discussing an author's workday and sharing her notebooks, original manuscripts, press sheets, and more. Students see how a professional writer follows the same creative process that they use, from idea gathering to final draft.

- Grade levels: K-5

- $

- *Flick on Trial.* WorryWart Publishing, 2000, ISBN 1881519120

  Flick. WorryWart Publishing, 1995, ISBN 1881519023

  The Prison Bird. WorryWart Publishing, 1991, ISBN 1881519015, International Graphic Arts Award 1991

Tennessee

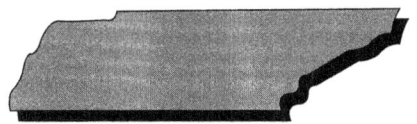

Tracy Barrett

PO Box 120061
Nashville, TN 37212
(615) 297-6785
scbwi.midsouth@juno.com
<www.redrival.com/mowrites4kids/usawrites4kids/barrett>

If a book has great characters, it's probably a great book. Using a series of writing exercises, Tracy Barrett helps students make their characters more vivid and exciting. She's been involved in many aspects of book production and shows kids the process of editing, which is especially useful for middle-school students, who often find the rewriting process tedious and discouraging. She also shows kids how illustrations are put to text and why books are published in page groupings that are multiples of eight.

- Grade levels: K-12
- $

Anna of Byzantium. Delacorte, 2000, ISBN 0440415365

Tennessee. Marshall Cavendish, 1997, ISBN 076140208X

Growing Up in Colonial America. Millbrook, 1995, ISBN 156294785

- Requirements: Overhead projector

Doris Gove

4204 Taliluna Avenue
Knoxville, TN 37919
(865) 522-9896
dorisgove@aol.com

Doris Gove enjoys sharing the process of writing, from rough draft (sloppy copy) to dummy, to full-sized print and finished book, with students. She integrates writing exercises into her program and reads from her books, all of which are about natural history.

- Grade levels: K-6
- $$

My Mother Talks to Trees. Peachtree, 1999, ISBN 1561451665

Red-Spotted Newt. Atheneum, 1994, ISBN 0689316976

Karen McIntyre

449 Cedarvalley Drive
Nashville, TN 37211
(615) 333-0626
kjmcinty@net-serv.com
<www.net-serv.com/mcintyre>

Storytelling is a means for people to explore their inner beliefs and the structure their world—we're story-formed people. Karen McIntyre uses storytelling to both heal and share the joy of life with listeners. In her presentation, she teaches the structure of good stories and helps students develop written or told stories, using cross-cultural and cross-generational examples.

- Grade levels: K-12
- $$

Vermont

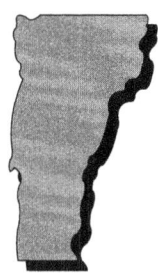

Susan Provost Beller

187 Stone Wall Lane
Charlotte, VT 05445-9324
(802) 425-2389
kidsbks@msn.com

What stories from history might make the past come alive for your students? Susan Beller offers several programs, ranging from the Civil and Revolutionary wars to more modern and personal history based on actual diaries, letters, and reminiscences that allow kids to become historians. She also offers programs to motivate kids to do research on their own topics, as well as genealogy programs and general talks on the writing process.

- Grade levels: 4-12
- $
- *Billy Yank and Johnny Reb: Soldiering in the Civil War.* Twenty-First Century, 2000, ISBN 0761318690

  Never Were Men So Brave: The Irish Brigade During the Civil War. McElderry, 1998, ISBN 0689814062

  To Hold This Ground: A Desperate Battle at Gettysburg. McElderry, 1995, ISBN 068950621x, Lupine Award Honor Book (Maine Library Association)

Tracey Campbell Pearson

PO Box 1114
Jericho Center, VT 05465
(802) 899-4991 phone/fax
pearsnvt@sover.net
<www.traceycampbellpearson.com>

A school visit from Tracey Campbell Pearson not only excites children about books and reading, but also plants an idea seed that they're artists and writers. Tracey begins by drawing for students, then takes them through the publishing process, from idea to finished book, using original artwork, sketches, dummies, final art, slides, proof sheets, and books.

- Grade levels: K-5
- $$
- *Awful Aardvarks Go to School.* By Reeve Lindbergh, Viking, 1997, ISBN 0670859206, 0140554482 pbk, *Booklist* starred review
- Requirements: Slide projector, screen, easel

Virginia

Laura J. Bobrow
102 Chesterfield Place SW
Leesburg, VA 20175-2700
eljbee@aol.com

From medieval troubadour to modern rap artist, experienced performers such as Laura Bobrow know that the art of telling a tale lies in the retelling. Students in her workshops approach a well-known tale from various directions to find its true voice without changing the basic motif. As kids tell their versions of a story, they learn to see and sense its characters and to connect with their feelings about it.

- Grade levels: 1-12

- $$

- *The Captain's Beard.* Riverbank Press, 1995, ISBN 0874067308

Muriel Miller Branch
9315 Radborne Road
Richmond, VA 23236
(804) 320-1765
(804) 320-2965 fax
mbranch@stories-plus.com
<www.stories-plus.com>

This storyteller's narrated slide presentations on African-American history and culture, including the Gullah, the history of Juneteenth, and stories of strong men and women, inspire students to be all they can be.

- Grade levels: 3-12

- $

- *Dear Ellen Bee: A Civil War Scrapbook of Two Union Spies.* Atheneum, 2000, ISBN 0689823797

  Juneteenth: Freedom Day. Cobblehill, 1998, ISBN 052565221

  The Water Brought Us: The Story of Two Gullah People. Cobblehill, 1995, ISBN 08684415300

Meredith Campbell
1104 Ironington Road
Richmond, VA 23227
(804) 264-2423 phone/fax
campbellrisen@juno.com
<www.authorsden.com>

Meredith Campbell, dressed in period clothing and affecting an Irish brogue, becomes "Dee Moone," a widowed, Irish, boarding-house keeper who lives in a border state during the Civil War and faces the problems of taking both sides. As "Sister Cecilia," Meredith becomes a medical nun who discusses hospital conditions during the conflict and tells of other nuns who served in the field.

- Grade levels: 4-12

- $

- *Haunted Warriors.* Two Trails, 2002, forthcoming

  Righteous Warriors. Two Trails Publishing, 2000, ISBN 1929311052

Ginjer L. Clarke

1633 Robindale Road
Richmond, VA 23235-4535
(804) 272-1312
(804) 272-4905 fax
ginjerc@aol.com
<www.elephanteditorial.com>

Sink your teeth into Ginjer Clarke's nonfiction animal books during her presentations, which provide kids with fun, fearsome facts. Her talks emphasize understanding and respecting animals, but also cover how books are made, as she shares her nonfiction titles and accompanying crafts with students.

- Grade levels: K-3
- $
- *Wild Dads!* Illustrated by Betina Ogden, Random House, 2002, ISBN 0375814493 pbk

  Sharks! Illustrated by Steven James Petruccio, Penguin Putnam, 2001, ISBN 0448425882, 0448424908 pbk

  Baby Alligator. Illustrated by Neecy Twinem, Penguin Putnam, 2000, ISBN 0448418517, 0448420953 pbk

- Requirements: Tables for craft workspace, crayons for kids

Pamela Duncan Edwards
(with illustrator Henry Cole)

1521 Windstone Drive
Vienna, VA 22182
(703) 759-5629
(703) 759-1192 fax
Pamaila@aol.com

Who's more important—the person who writes the words or the person who draws the pictures? Author Pamela Duncan Edwards and illustrator Henry Cole humorously sort out this dilemma and make children take sides, but finally teaching them valuable lessons about collaboration. Students learn that getting everything right the first time is rare, and that to do a good job means being willing to do things over and over until it's right. Pamela and Henry also involve kids in producing a page of one of their working manuscripts.

- Grade levels: K-6
- $-$$$$
- *Warthogs in the Kitchen: A Messy Color Book.* Hyperion, 1998, ISBN 07868-03991, *Publishers Weekly* starred review, Parents' Choice recommendation, International Reading Association/Children's Book Council Children's Choice

  Dinorella: A Prehistoric Fairy Tale. Hyperion, 1997, ISBN 0786803036, National Council of Teachers of English Notable Book

  Livingstone Mouse. HarperCollins, 1996, ISBN 0060258691, California Young Readers' Medal 1998-9

- Requirements: Table, two chairs, large easel, drawing pad

Linda Goodman

PO Box 1351
Chesterfield, VA 23832-1351
(804) 778-7456
happytales@aol.com
<www.lindagoodmanstoryteller.com>

Linda Goodman, an Appalachian Mountains native of Melungeon descent, is described as one of the great living masters of the storytelling art. She combines original and traditional tales and teaches workshops on family stories, cultural integrity, and how to make full stories from fragments. Her programs include *A Little Bit of Kindness, Daughters of the Appalachians,* and *Scenes from the Dim Smoky Past.* She's the recipient of the Southern Connecticut State University's Excellence in Storytelling Award and a 1998 *Storytelling World* Honor Award.

- Grade levels: 3-12
- $-$$
- *Daughters of the Appalachians.* Overmountain Press, ISBN 1570720983

Jacqueline Jules

2800 North Dinwiddie Street
Arlington, VA 22207
(703) 237-9617
JacJules@aol.com

Jacqueline Jules, a poet, an author, a singer, and a storyteller, entertains young audiences with stories, songs, puppets, poetry, finger plays, and flannel-board activities. Participatory stories are her specialty, as are stories, songs, and art for Jewish holidays.

- Grade levels: K-6
- $
- *The Hardest Word: A Yom Kippur Story.* Illustrations by Katherine Janus Kahn, Kar-Ben Copies, 2001, ISBN 1580130305, 1580130283 pbk

  Clap and Count: Action Rhymes for the Jewish Year. Kar-Ben Copies, 2001, ISBN 1580130674

  Once Upon a Shabbos. Kar-Ben Copies, 1998, ISBN 1580130208, 1580130216 pbk, Sugarman Family Award

Joan Leotta

9728 Stipp Street
Burke, VA 22015
(703) 455-4711
JGL1@aol.com
<www.voicesintheglen.org/tellers/jleotta>

Joan Leotta performs folktales, dragon stories, dinosaur tales, and Aesop's and Greek myths, as well as stories from American history and from African, Asian, South and Central American, Arab, and Hispanic cultures. Throw in a few tall tales, and you've got the gist of her presentation. Joan also assumes the costumed characters of Narcissa Whitman, an indentured servant on the Westward trail, and of a whaler's wife.

- Grade levels: K-8
- $$
- *Massachusetts.* Grolier/Scholastic, 2001, ISBN 0516224867

  Tales as Tools (2 chapters). Riverbank Press, 1994, ISBN 1877991152
- Requirements: Table, chair, sound system

Kathy L. May

495 Underhill Lane
Charlottesville, VA 22911
kmay2k@earthlink.net
<www.usawrites4kids.drury.edu/authors/may>

Kathy May uses her book to show younger students how to act out the story, with costumes and props. For older students, she shows slides of field research and of book parts and revisions, and discusses writing and publishing. She also teaches poetry and fiction writing for older students. She shows molasses-making tools and cane stalks, and offers molasses treats, to all ages.

- Grade levels: K-12
- $
- *Molasses Man.* Holiday House, 2000, ISBN 0823414388

Elaine Moore

420 Ole Dirt Road
Great Falls, VA 22066
(703) 444-3499 or (800) 597-2043
(703) 404-2010 fax
Elaine@elainemoore.com
<www.elainemoore.com>

Elaine Moore's nationally acclaimed *Under the Purple Writer's Hat* programs feature color graphics that appeal to diverse audiences with various learning styles. Her popular *Pizza! Workshop* helps students with the difficult revision process. In *Add-a-word Pizza*, she helps children embellish a simple sentence until it's surprising and interesting. In *Stories Alive*, she guides students through an ever-changing story plot.

- Grade levels: K-6
- $$$
- Requirements: Sound system, overhead projector, screen, chalkboard or chart paper

Barbara Ann Porte

PO Box 16627
Arlington, VA 22215

Barbara Porte is a children's librarian-turned-storyteller who's told stories, presented programs, lectured, and taught writing in schools, museums, libraries, and universities. She's won American Library Association Notable awards, Young Adult Best Books of the Year citations, the American Booksellers Association Pick of the Lists, and many other awards.

- Grade levels: K-12

- $-$$

- *If You Ever Get Lost: The Adventures of Julia and Evan.* Illustrated by Nancy Carpenter, Greenwillow, 2000, ISBN 0688169473

  Ma Jiang and the Orange Ants. Illustrated by Annie Cannon, Scholastic, 2000, ISBN 0531302415

Candice Ransom

6819 Orchid Lane
Fredericksburg, VA 22407
(540) 786-8382
xencfr@infi.net

The author of more than six dozen books for children and a seasoned speaker, Candice Ransom offers several programs, including *The Ghost of Gertrude Warner* (author of the *Boxcar Children* series), *Adventures as a Ghostwriter, How I Became a Writer,* and the *A Day in the Life of an Author* slide show. Candice also speaks on *History as Adventure* (about writing historical fiction) and gives presentations on growing up on battlefields and real children during the Civil War. She also conducts writing workshops.

- Grade levels: K-12

- $$

- *The Big Green Pocketbook.* HarperCollins, 1993, ISBN 0-06020849x

Rosalyn Schanzer

11630 Havenner Road
Fairfax Station, VA 22039
(703) 425-5820
(703) 425-3774 fax
schanze@attglobal.net

Rosalyn Schanzer's informative and humorous performances share her meticulous research on Lewis and Clark, the California Gold Rush, and American immigration. Her storytelling is done in costume and with lots of audience participation.

- Grade levels: K-6

- $

- *Davy Crockett Saves the World.* HarperCollins, 2001, ISBN 0688169910, *Booklist* Editor's Choice, American Library Association starred review, Oppenheim Portfolio Best Book Award

  The Old Chisholm Trail, A Cowboy Song. National Geographic Society, 2001, ISBN 0792275594, National Association of Parenting Publications Silver Award, Texas Book Festival presentation selection

  How We Crossed the West: The Adventures of Lewis and Clark. National Geographic Society, 1997, ISBN 0792237382, National Council for Social Studies Notable Trade Book, *School Library Journal* starred review, *Publishers Weekly* starred review

- Requirements: Slide projector, screen, sound system

Heather L. Tomasello

4909 Merlin Lane
Glen Allen, VA 23060
(804) 747-5565
reiscake@ufl.edu
<www.sciencefairstrategies.com>

What's green, glowing, and growing on that science fair project? What does it really mean to "mind your p's and q's"? How does one get into and pay for college? Heather Tomasello answers these questions and more during her presentations. As a teen, she won national recognition at science fairs and in writing competitions, and funded her college education completely with scholarships. She's worked as an academic advisor and writing coach, as well as being an author.

- Grade levels: 2-12

- $

- *So, You Have to Do a Science Fair Project.* Wiley & Sons, 2002, ISBN 0471202568

  Strategies for Winning Science Fair Projects. Wiley & Sons, 2001, ISBN 0471419575

Jim Weiss

Greathall Productions
PO Box 5061
Charlottesville, VA 22905-5061
(800) 477-6234
(434) 296-4490 fax
greathall@greathall.com
<www.greathall.com>

Literature comes alive with Jim Weiss. From fairy tales and Shakespeare to the ancient world of Greek mythology or the mystique of Sherlock Holmes, Jim's performances delight and entertain all ages. He also teaches storytelling and story writing to all ages. Jim has dozens of recordings on numerous topics, and many of the recordings have received awards from the American Library Association, the Oppenheim Toy Portfolio, the Parents' Choice Foundation, *AudioFile* magazine, *Storytelling World* magazine, and the National Association of Parenting Publications.

- Grade levels: K-12

- $

- *Tell Me a Story: A Treasury of Classics.* Greathall, 2001, ISBN 1882513770 CD, 1882513255 cassette

  Treasure Island. Greathall, 2001, ISBN 1882513762 CD, 1882513517 cassette

  Jewish Holiday Stories. Greathall, 2001, ISBN 1882513754 CD

Washington, D.C.

Mary Quattlebaum

c/o Random House Children's Books
1540 Broadway, 20th Floor
New York, NY 10036
<www.maryq\ebaum.com>

Where do you get ideas? How are books made? Do poems have to rhyme? Kids are full of questions and often eager to pen their own stories and poems. Mary Quattlebaum's interactive presentations show her process, from draft to illustrator's sketches to finished book, and may include crafts, sound, music, and creative movement. This award-winning author (*Marguerite de Angeli*, Blue Ribbon from Children's Book Council, Sugarman Award) of picture books, novels, and poetry also can guide young writers in special workshops on writing.

- Grade levels: K-6

- $$

- *The Shine Man.* Eerdmans, 2001, ISBN 0802851819

    Grover G. Graham and Me. Random House/Delacorte, 2001, ISBN 0385322771

    Underground Train. Random House/Doubleday, 1997, ISBN 0440413257

Scott Sedar

4345 Ellicott Street NW
Washington, DC 20016
(202) 966-4778
(202) 966-3454 fax
bsedar@aol.com

Scott Sedar's various programs explore music, geometry, and time to teach rhythm and history. His exploration of these concepts with students uses a variety of shapes, sounds, and instruments, including Scott himself. He has been an artist in residence at the Kennedy Center and has won a Bronze medal from the New York Film Festival for his video script of *Sudden Infant Death Syndrome* (1990).

- Grade levels: 1-6

- $

- Requirements: An open area where children can move and dance

West Virginia

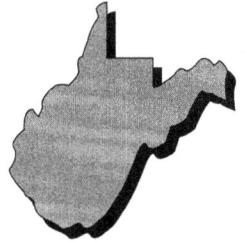

Jo Ann Dadisman

Route 1, Box 69A
Independence, WV 26374
(304) 864-6861
(304) 864-0879 fax
jdadisman@aol.com

Part of the Mountain Echoes tandem tellers, Jo Ann Dadisman shares true stories, traditional tales from the West Virginia mountains, and stories that help students know and understand themselves.

- Grade levels: K-12
- $

Connie Donovan

230 Hillcrest Road
Weirton, WV 26062
(304) 797-9604

Amusing storyteller Connie Donovan reads tales she's written and promotes active participation in stories that spur the imagination.

- Grade levels: K-5
- $

Andy Fraenkel

RD1 NBU 19
Moundsville, WV 26041
(304) 845-6840
story108@juno.com

Andy Fraenkel's programs take an ordinary space and transform it into something magical by weaving together his gifts as a storyteller, an author, and an actor. He uses stories and music from many lands to promote positive values, an appreciation for world literature, and creative self-expression in students. His workshops for older students and adults explore the art of theater and storytelling. Andy's the National Storytelling Network liaison for West Virginia, a performing arts specialist at Towngate Theater, and a cofounder of A Voice We Bring.

- Grade levels: K-12
- $
- *The Rime of the Ancient Mariner: A Retelling.* Multicultural Stories Network, 1999, ISBN 0932215351

  The Fish Who Wouldn't Stop Growing: Twelve Stories from Ancient India. Multicultural Stories Network, 1995, ISBN 0932215343

  Sacred Voices: A Pilgrimage into the World's Traditions. Cassette, self-published, no ISBN

Bill Hairston

PO Box 4466
Owens Station
Charleston, WV 25364
(304) 925-8792
(801) 991-8929 fax
bhairston@ntelos.net

Humorist Bill Hairston's stories and music are based on his experiences growing up in rural West Virginia, along the Coal River. His stories embody the area's rich, Appalachian culture and the contributions of African Americans to Appalachian history.

- Grade levels: K-12
- $
- *Nobody Knows.* 1995, cassette, self-published, no ISBN
- Requirements: Sound system

Susanna "Granny Sue" Holstein

Route 2, Box 110
Sandyville, WV 25275
(877) 459-5502 (toll free)
holstein_susanna@hotmail.com
<www.wvstorytelling.com>

Stories from the Mountains and Beyond showcases Granny Sue's experiences as a mother, a sister, a wife, a grandmother, a farmer, a security guard, a mail carrier, a betting clerk, a teacher, and a librarian. Her stories are drawn from Appalachian lore and the treasury of world folktales, as well as her own life. Whether she's telling ghost stories, folktales, personal stories, or downright lies, Granny Sue is enjoyed by audience of all ages.

- Grade levels: K-12
- $

June Riffel

Route 6, Box 161-B
Fairmont, WV 26554
(304) 367-1724
jeriffle@aol.com

Part of the Mountain Echoes tandem tellers, June Riffel shares true stories, traditional tales from the West Virginia mountains, and stories that help students know and understand themselves.

- Grade levels: K-12
- $

Karen Vuranch

PO Box 383
Fayetteville, WV 25840
(304) 574-4840
wventerprises@inetone.net
<www.wventerprises.com>

Karen Vuranch weaves together a love of history, a passion for stories, and a sense of community to entertain listeners and empower them to find their own stories. Karen tells traditional Appalachian, Celtic, multicultural, and spooky tales. She performs with The Old Time Travelers, accompanied by Laura Davis and Gary Reynolds (on fiddle and banjo/guitar), and has toured internationally with *Coal Camp Memories,* which dramatizes life in the Appalachian coalfields. She also performs living history characters such as Pearl Buck (writer), Mother Jones (labor organizer), Mary Draper Ingles (Indian captive), Emma Edmonds (Civil War soldier and spy), and Clara Barton (humanitarian), as well as *Homefront,* a one-woman play about WWII.

- Grade levels: K-12
- $
- *My Grandmother's Necklace and Other Stories.* CRT Co., 2000, cassette, no ISBN
- Requirements: Wireless microphone

Wisconsin

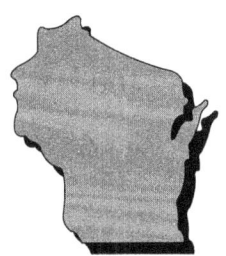

Sharon Hart Addy

4098 East Studio Lane
Oak Creek, WI 53145
(414) 764-3666

What does it mean to be an author? Sharon Addy's *Right Here* presentation explains it all to kids by combining lively entertainment with an appreciation for digging for facts and other valuables lost to the wiles of time. Sharon also leads creative writing workshops for all ages.

- Grade levels: K-12
- $
- *When Wishes Were Horses.* Illustrated by Brad Sneed, Houghton Mifflin, 2001, ISBN 0618131663

  Right Here on This Spot. Illustrated by John Clapp, Houghton Mifflin, 1999, ISBN 0395730910, Archer/Eckbald Children's Picture Book Award, Outstanding Achievement in Children's Literature by the Wisconsin Library Association

  Kidding Around Milwaukee. John Muir/Avon Travel, 1997, ISBN 1562613626
- Requirements: Chalk- or whiteboard, table

Diane L. Burns

4099 North Shore Drive
Rhinelander, WI 54401
(715) 32-5338
(800) 737-9787

Diane Burns's *Best-Kept Fiction Writer's Secret* workshop adds pizzazz to young writers' work by using snippets of Sendak, Paterson, and Paulsen (among others). She also offers *Cooking Up a Story,* which draws the analogy between pie making and story making with dialogue, setting, and conflict as part of the recipe. In her *Superwriter* workshop, she discusses the power of words and shows a simple technique for making writing stronger. Diane's been an instructor for the Institute of Children's Literature for many years, as well as a forest service fire lookout.

- Grade levels: K-8
- $$
- *Take Along Guide* series (five titles). Gareth Stevens, 2000, various ISBNs

  Plant a Garden in Your Sneaker. McGraw-Hill, 1998, ISBN 0070092281

  Cranberries: Fruit of the Bog. Carolrhoda, 1994, ISBN 0876148224, 0876119646 pbk

Jean-Andrew Dickman

6023 W. Lincoln Avenue
Milwaukee, WI 53219
(414) 327-1877
(414) 327-7355 fax
jean-andrew@juno.com

Rekindle your imagination with this seasoned storyteller, educator, and elementary school librarian. Jean-Andrew Dickman has a lively and engaging style, and her programs draw on a wide range of tales, including holiday tales, spiritual stories, global folktales, life tales, and book tales. She also teaches graduate courses in storytelling, is the cofounder of the Milwaukee Area Storytellers Guild, and is the winner of the 1999 Lucy Beck Award for storytelling.

- Grade levels: K-12
- $

- *Twittertales.* Cassette, self-published, no date, no ISBN

  Storylore. Cassette, self-published, no date, no ISBN

  Earlybird Stories. Cassette, self-published, no date, no ISBN

R. Hardy Garrison

PO Box 792
Madison, WI 53701-0792
(608) 244-9165
hardy@storyguy.com
<www.storyguy.com>
info@wistory.org
<www.WIStory.org>

All ages delight in Hardy Garrison's rollicking retellings of folktales from around the globe. Hardy's enthusiastic and humorous telling style is often infused with a healthy dose of audience participation. In addition to stories on a wide range of topics, he also offers storytelling workshops to get beginners started.

- Grade levels: K-6
- $

John D. Ivanko

7843 County Road P
Browntown, WI 53522
(608) 329-7056
(608) 329-7057 fax
john@innserendipity.com
<www.innserendipity.com/kid/kidauthor.html>

Join John Ivanko as he takes listeners around the world and celebrates diversity during his hands-on workshop, *Passport to the World,* in which kids pass through customs of various countries. He also offers slide programs, *PhotoQuest* and *Xanadu,* in which kids paint or draw an imaginary country, and *My Press Pass,* which turns kids into backyard journalists.

- Grade levels: K-12
- $

- *To Be a Kid.* Charlesbridge, 1999, ISBN 0881068411, National Association for the Education of Young Children Directors Choice Award, National Council for Social Studies/Children's Book Council Notable Social Studies Trade Book, National Parenting Center Seal of Approval

  Back to School: It's a Kid's World series. Charlesbridge, 2002, ISBN 1570913838

  Animal Friends. Charlesbridge, 2002, ISBN 1570915024

- Requirements: Slide projector

Janet Jensen

4835 Easy Street, #2
Hartland, WI 53029
(262) 367-3392
janetmjensen@hotmail.com

Janet Jensen tells folk and personal tales, plays guitar, and sings, and often does tandem storytelling with her husband.

- Grade levels: K-12
- $
- Requirements: Sound system

Bob Jensen

4835 Easy Street, #2
Hartland, WI 53029
(262) 367-3392
rjensen@compaq.net

Bob Jensen is a Presbyterian pastor who incorporates stories of faith in his performances, both in and beyond the church setting. He often tells in tandem with his librarian wife.

- Grade levels: K-12
- $
- Requirements: Sound system

Bob Kann

462 Marston Avenue
Madison, WI 53703
(608) 257-0958
bobkann@charter.net
<www.bobkann.com>

Bob Kann offers storytelling, magic, and juggling shows that specialize in comedy, audience participation, and making literature come alive. He also performs programs on themes such as *Read-Read-Read, Save the Cranes: Protecting an Endangered Species, If I Were a Building: Frank Lloyd Wright,* and *Architecture.* Invite Bob to your school and find out how Dincerella slopped her dripper and why a frog's favorite cereal is Toadal!

Grade levels: K-8

$

Amy C. Laundrie

918 Pine Dive
Wisconsin Dells, WI 53965
(608) 254-8426
laundrie@midplains.net
<www.laundrie.com>

Amy Laundrie plays a writing game called *What If?* with students in which they use their imaginations and learn how books begin. She also uses a slide presentation with older students to detail the writing process and discusses how her interests and passions direct her novels.

Grade levels: 3-7

$

Wolves in Sheep's Clothing. Royal Fireworks, 2001, ISBN 088092543

Eye of Truth. Royal Fireworks, 1996, ISBN 088923040

Thirty Pieces of Silver. Royal Fireworks 1996, ISBN 0880923644

Marybeth Lorbiecki

210 Seventh Street North
Hudson, WI 54016
mlorb@redwing.net

Marybeth Lorbiecki gives lively school presentations on the life of Aldo Leopold, the seasonal life of the Dakota Sioux, and the life of Dr. Charles Eastman, who was formative in the Boy Scouts and Campfire Girls. She also leads workshops on writing, which include giving young writers a behind-the-scenes look at the process of building a book from an idea.

Grade levels: K-12

$$

Louisa May and Mr. Thoreau's Flute. Coauthored with Julie Dunlap, illustrated by Mary Azarian, Dial, 2002, ISBN 0803724705, Junior Library Guild selection

Painting the Dakota: Seth Eastman at Fort Snelling. Illustrated with paintings by Seth Eastman, Afton Historical Society Press, 2000, ISBN 1890434329, Ben Franklin Award for Juvenile Literature

Sister Anne's Hands. Illustrated by Wendy Popp, Dial, 1999, ISBN 0803720386, 0140565345 pbk, International Reading Association Storyteller World Award, Bank Street College Best Books of the Year Award, Notable Trade Book for Young People, numerous other awards

JoAnn Early Macken

4462 North Newhall Street
Shorewood, WI 53211
(414) 332-22359
macken@wi.rr.com

JoAnn Macken offers a workshop titled *Write a Poem Step by Step* that teaches kids how to use imagery, exciting words, and form to create a poem. She also conducts workshops on haiku, rhyme, limericks, and shape poems that cover getting ideas, incorporating imagery, writing with exciting words, and finding the right form for a poem. JoAnn was the winner of the Barbara Juster Esbensen Poetry Teaching Award in 2000.

- Grade levels: K-12
- $
- *Cats on Judy.* Whispering Coyote, 1997, ISBN 1879085739

  Animal Worlds series. Gareth Stevens Publishing, various ISBNs

Peter and Connie Roop

2601 North Union
Appleton, WI 54911-2141
(920) 731-5364
peterroop@aol.com

The Roop's program, *The Story of a Story,* traces the creation of a Roop book, from idea through the writing process to final publication. Using their combined decades of classroom experience and their background of coauthoring 75 books, Peter and Connie connect with students, inspiring them to become better writers. The duo also relates what they do as "adult" writers with what young authors can do. In addition, the Roops offer poetry and journal-writing workshops.

- Grade levels: K-8
- $$
- *Buffalo Jump.* Northland, 1994, ISBN 0873587316

  Keep the Light Burning, Abbie. Carolrhoda, 1987, ISBN 0876144547

  Girl of the Shining Mountains: Sacajawea's Story. Hyperion, 1999, ISBN 078604920
- Requirements: Carousel slide projector

Pattima Singhalaka

Guppy Design
2912 Edgewood Drive, Apt. #2
Menomonie, WI 54751
(715) 233-0284 phone/fax
darthguppy@charter.net
darthguppy@hotmail.com
<www.portfolios.com/guppyillustration>

In her presentations, Pattima Singhalaka tells Thai stories and folktales from the world, and talks about the art of making art, with a drawing and painting demonstration. She also enjoys discussing book arts, helping students be creatively involved in turning events from their lives into stories, and talking about the business of illustration and writing.

- Grade levels: K-12
- $
- *Starduster.* Moon Mountain Publishing, 2001, ISBN 0967792940
- Requirements: Computer projector, screen

Marsha Valance

343 North 62nd Street
Milwaukee, WI 53213-4130
(414) 607-0288
tributefarm@mixcom.com
<www.angelfire.com/wi/tributefarm/storytel.htm>

Marsha Valance specializes in fairy tales, fantasy, folklore, personal stories, and oral history during her animated, participatory storytelling sessions. She's the past president of the Northlands Storytelling Network and founder of the Grand Rapids Storytelling festival.

- Grade levels: K-12
- $
- Requirements: Sound system

Karen M. Wendt

1218 South Thompson Drive
Madison, WI 53716
(608) 222-0512
bewendt@facstaff.wisc.edu

Karen Wendt's fast-paced program of folktales, fables, and animal tales from around the world challenges listeners to toss their nets into the sky, catch a story, let it go, and share it. Karen also performs "instant theater," using puppets and children from the audience, and offers a wild workshop called *Lions! Tigers! Snakes! and Whales!,* in which she blends face painting with storytelling.

- Grade levels: K-5
- $

Jim Winship

184 North Franklin Street
Whitewater, WI 53190
(262) 473-3381
winshipj@mail.uww.edu

Jim Winship tells bilingual (English and Spanish) stories of wizardry, magical tales where reality takes a sharp turn, and personal stories, and teaches students how storytelling can sharpen their writing skills.

- Grade levels: 1-12
- $
- Requirements: Cordless mike

Resources: Cyber and Others

Talent in Cyberspace

Just as everyone on the streets of Los Angeles is writing a screenplay, everyone in the performing world is developing a Web site. Using your favorite search engine by simply using a person's name as the keywords usually will get you to that person's home page. The gateways listed below host a wide variety of authors, illustrators, and storytellers.

Gateways

<www.abfc.com> (Association of Booksellers for Children)
<www.artcyclopedia.com> (artists)
<www.authorsguild.org>
<www.carolhurst.com>
<www.cbcbook.org/> (Children's Book Council)
<www.childrenslit.com>
<www.cynthialeitichsmith.com>
<www.falcon.jmu.edu/>
<www.frsd.k12.nj.us/barleylibrary/author>
<www.goodconversations.com>
<www.iwwg.com> (International Women's Writing Guild)
<www.kidsread.com>
<www.lib.usm.edu/~degrum/>
<www.people.virginia.edu/~jbh/author.html>
<www.readin.org> (Read In Foundation)
<www.scbwi.org>
<www.storybookart.com>
<www.storynet.org>
<www.thebestkidsbooksite.com>
<www.ucalgary.ca/~dkbrown/authors>
<usawrites4kids.drury.edu>
<www.womenwritingthewest.org>

Storytellers

Hint: When searching the Web for storytellers' sites, use keywords "storyteller" and "directory."

<www.storytnet.org/> (National Storytellers Association)
<www.storytellingcenter.com>
<www.edupaperback.org/> (many authors)
<storytellers-hanksville.org/storytellers>
<www.nobs.org/> (Network of Biblical Storytellers)
<www.activated-storytellers.com>
<www.blackstorytellers.com>
<www.nhhc.org> (Chautauqua performers)
<www.ccnet.com> (California Indian Storytellers Association)
<www.youthstorytelling.com> (for youngsters who want to learn how to tell stories)
<www.storysaac.org> (Storytelling Association of Alta, CA)
<www.storyfest.com> (Bob and Kelly Wilhem)

Other Resources

Schoolvisit.net

4306 Brookwoods
Houston, TX 77092
(713) 480-7069
woodtee@aol.com
<www.schoolvisit.net>

Vuthy Kuon offers authors, storytellers, illustrators, and other talented performers a free listing on the site, where teachers and librarians who are seeking visiting performers may find them.

Costume Specialists

211 North Fifth Avenue
Columbus, OH 43215
(800) 596-9357
(614) 464-2114 fax
info@cospec.com

Did you ever wonder where those huge Clifford, Franklin, Spot, Pinkerton, and Curious George costumes come from? This is where.

Society of Children's Book Writers and Illustrators

8271 Beverly Boulevard
Los Angeles, CA 90048
(323) 782-1010
(323) 782-1892 fax
scbwi@scbwi.org
<www.scbwi.org>

Members receive monthly updates; e-mail information about publishers and authors; and annual directories of publishers of books for young people, complete with addresses, contact people, and more. Also available is a directory of authors, illustrators, and others. Published authors have full membership, others are associate members; both memberships cost $60 a year.

National Storytelling Association

101 Courthouse Square
Jonesborough, TN 37659
(800) 525-4514 toll free
(423) 913-8201
(423) 753-9331 fax
<nsnanaxs.net>

Children's Book Council

12 West 37th Street
New York, NY 10018-7480
(212) 966-1990
(212) 966-2073 fax
<www.cbcbooks.org>

Providing fantastic links to publishers, authors, publications, and bibliographies, this nonprofit trade organization is dedicated to children's books and is the official sponsor of Children's Book Week and Young People's Poetry Week.

Northlands Storytelling Network

PO Box 1055
McHenry, IL 60051
info@northlands.net

Children's Book Guild of Washington, D.C.

<Childrensbookguild.org>

The Guild is made up of authors, illustrators, and children's literature specialists who meet monthly to set high standards for children's books and to increase knowledge and use of better books for children. The names of current members who make school visits can be found on the Web site.

Storytellers: A Biographical Directory of 120 English-Speaking Performers Worldwide. By Corki Miller & Mary Ellen Snodgrass, McFarland & Co., 1998, ISBN 0786404701

Index by Performer

Authors

Abbott, Tony, 13
Addy, Sharon Hart, 141
Adler, David, 83
Adlerman, Danny, 75
Adlerman, Kim, 75
Alder, Elizabeth, 111
Alko, Selina, 83
Allen, Mary Emma, 71
Anderson, Mike, 33
Anzalotti, Pamela, 33
Appleton, Betty, 63

Backtalk Productions, 87
Baldwin, Robert, 45
Ball, Liz, 111
Barchers, Suzanne, 13
Barkin, Carol, 83
Barrett, Tracy, 127
Bart, Kathleen, 84
Baskin, Nora Raleigh, 13
Baumgartner, Barbara, 115
Bea, Holly, 21
Beatty, Monica Driscoll, 53
Beckhorn, Susan Williams, 84
Bellavia, Timothy, 84
Beller, Susan Provost, 129
Belviso, Meg, 101
Berkes, Marianne, 21
Billingsley, Franny, 33
Birch, Carol, 14
Black, Judith, 53
Blatchford, Claire, 54
Bobrow, Laura, 131
Bodkin, Odds, 71
Bogar, Tim, 63
Bolley, Jean, 63
Bowen, Fred, 49
Bradbury, Judy, 84
Branch, Muriel Miller, 131

Brennan, Linda Crotta, 121
Brewster, Patience, 85
Brill, Marlene Targ, 34
Brisson, Pat, 75
Brody, Janis, 85
Broerman, Joan, 11
Brown, Roberta Simpson, 43
Bruchac, James, 85
Bruchac, Joseph, 85
Buchanan, Jane, 115
Burns, Diane, 141
Burns, Phyllis Ann, 34
Butts, Ellen, 49
Buzzeo, Toni, 45

Cabral, Len, 121
Calmenson, Stephanie, 86
Campbell, Meredith, 131
Capucilli, Alyssa Satin, 86
Carson, Rick, 111
Caseley, Judith, 86
Chappas, Bess, 29
Choi, Yangsook, 87
Clarke, Ginjer, 132
Clayson, Jill, 87
Cleary, Brian, 112
Cleary, Rita, 87
Clements, Jehan, 87
Clifton, Sharon Kirk, 41
Cobb, Vicki, 88
Cohen, Caron Lee, 88
Collier, James Lincoln, 88
Collins, David, 34
Collins, Pat Lowery, 54
Corey, Shana, 88
Crimi, Carolyn, 34
Crompton, Laurie Ann, 89
Cruzan, Patricia, 29
Cummings, Priscilla, 49
Cusack, Margaret, 89
Cuyler, Margery, 76
Czarnota, Lorna McDonald, 89

Dadisman, Jo Ann, 139
Dafydd the Storyteller, 46
Dague, James, 35
Daniels, Teri, 89
Davidson, Robert, 45
Davies, Jacqueline, 54
Davis, Frances, 109
Davis, Gibbs, 90
Davis, Katie, 91
Davis, Myra, 21
Davol, Marguerite, 54
Demarest, Chris, 71
Derby, Ken, 22
DeSpain, Pleasant, 90
Dick, Linda, 63
Dickman, Jean-Andrew, 141
Dodge, Christopher Jay, 64
Donahue, Shari Faden, 115
Donlon, Diane Youngblood, 64
Donovan, Connie, 139
Dooley, Norah, 55
Dooling, Michael, 76
Dubisch, Carolyn Watson, 90

Eagle, Kin, 75
Edwards, Pamela Duncan, 132
Einhorn, Edward, 90
Ellis, Brian "Fox", 35
Ellis, Sid "The Rock", 64
Elster, Jean Alicia, 64

Faine, Edward Allen, 50
Farnsworth, Bill, 22
Feder, Harriet, 91
Feeney, Betsy Franco, 91
Feeney, Kathy, 22
Fehler, Gene, 125
Fincken, Hank, 41
Finkelstein, Norman, 55
Fletcher, Ralph, 72
Foland, Constance, 91

Fradin, Judith Bloom, 35
Fraenkel, Andy, 139
Francis, Michael, 55
Fraustino, Lisa Rowe, 14
Freeman, Marcia, 22
Frost, Helen, 41
Furstinger, Nancy, 92

Gail, Judy, 23
Gantos, Jack, 55
Garden, Nancy, 56
Garrison, R. Hardy, 142
Gay, Kathlyn, 23
Ghigna, Charles, 11
Gibson, Drew, 14
Gibson, Kathleen, 35
Glaser, Michael, 56
Goldman, Dara, 56
Golembe, Carla, 50
Goodman, Linda, 132
Gorham, Linda, 36
Gormley, Beatrice, 57
Gorog, Judith, 116
Gove, Doris, 127
Green, Michelle, 50
Greenberg, Melanie Hope, 92
Greenburg, Bonnie, 57
Greenburg, Dan, 92
Greenburg, Judith 92
Greene, Rhonda Gowler, 64
Greenstein, Elaine, 93
Gryniewicz, Gene, 36
Gutman, Dan, 76

Hairston, Bill, 139
Hall, Elizabeth, 93
Hansen, Sandra, 65
Haskins, Jim, 93
Hathaway, Lucinda, 23
Hausman, Gerald, 24
Hawkins, Suzette, 125
Healy, Yvonne, 65
Heusler, Marianna, 94
High, Linda Oatman, 116

Himmelman, John, 15
Hirschfelder, Arlene, 76
Holm, Jennifer, 94
Holstein, Susanna "Granny Sue", 140
Howard, Elizabeth, Fitzgerald, 116
Hubbell, Patricia, 15
Huling, Jan, 77
Huling, Phil, 77
Hurwitz, Johanna, 94

Intrater, Roberta Grobel, 94
Ivanko, John, 142

Jacobson, Jennifer Richard, 46
Jango-Cohen, Judith, 57
Janovitz, Marilyn, 95
Jensen, Bob, 142
Jensen, Janet, 142
Jocelyn, Marthe, 95
Johnson, Dinah, 125
Johnson, Leanne, 36
Johnson-Webb, Anna, 36
Jones, Marcia Thornton, 43
Jones, Ron, 109
Jules, Jacqueline, 132
Juster, Norton, 57

Kaighn, Laura, 77
Kammeraad, Kevin, 65
Kann, Bob, 143
Karr, Susan Schott, 77
Karwoski, Gail Lerner, 29
Katz, Bobbi, 95
Kay, Alan, 24
Keehn, Sally, 117
Kemba, Momma, 36
Kennedy, Mary, 19
Kenyon, Ross, 72
Kichler, Florrie Binford, 42
Kilborne, Sarah, 95
Kinsella, Marilyn, 37
Kittinger, Jo, 11
Kjelle, Marylou Moran, 77
Klingler, Angela Cay, 72
Koller, Jackie French, 58

Korman, Gordon, 96
Krensky, Stephen, 58
Kroll, Steven, 96
Kudlinski, Kathleen, 15
Kummer, Patricia, 37

Ladd, Louise, 15
Lalli, Judy, 117
Land, Karen, 96
Landau, Elaine, 24
Lanton, Sandy, 78
Lanza, Barbara, 96
Larkin, Chuck, 30
Laundrie, Amy, 143
Leotta, Joan, 133
Lessac, Frané, 78
Lessem, Don, 58
Leventhal, Rona, 59
Levinson, Marilyn, 97
Levitt, Marc Joel, 121
Lewis, E.B., 78
Lies, Brian, 59
Lint, David, 46
Lipke, Barbara, 59
Livingstone, Star, 97
Long, Kathy, 117
Lorbiecki, Marybeth, 143
Lovejoy, Sharon, 46
Lubar, David, 117
Luke, Linda, 65
Luthardt, Kevin, 37
Lynn, Paddy, 37

MacDonald, Amy, 46
Macintosh, Brownie, 72
Mackall, Dandi Daley, 112
Macken, JoAnn Early, 143
Macy, Sue, 79
Maestro, Betsy, 16
Maestro, Giulio, 16
Mallen, Lisa, 37
Marcello, Patricia Cronin, 24
Marston, Elsa, 42
Marston, Hope Irvin, 97

Martia, Dominic, 25
Marx, Trish, 97
Masoff, Joy, 98
Masters, Susan Rowan, 98
Matero, Robert, 79
May, Kathy, 133
Mazer, Anne, 98
McCabe, Tom, 59
McDonald, Joyce, 79
McGovern, Ann, 98
McIntyre, Karen, 127
McMillan, Bruce, 47
Meacham, Margaret, 51
Miller, Bobbi, 16
Miller, Brandon Marie, 112
Miller, Candace, 113
Miller, Genia, 87
Miller, Maryjane, 38
Moffatt, Judith, 60
Moore, Elaine, 133
Moore, MariJo, 109
Moore, Robin, 118
Mora, Pat, 43
Morse, Andy, 99
Mueller, Pamela Bauer, 30
Munro, Roxie, 99
Myers, Laurie, 30

Neitzel, Shirley, 66
Nelson, Ann Gieseler Bryan, 66
NeSmith, Phyllis, 21
Newman, Aline Alexander, 99
Nobisso, Josephine "Joi", 99
Nobleman, Marc Tyler, 100
Noonan, Julia, 100
Norfolk, Sherry, 30

O'Connell, Rebecca, 118
O'Connor, Barbara, 60

Packie, Tammy, 47
Park, Linda Sue, 100
Parker, Barbara Keevil, 122
Pearl, Sydelle, 60
Pearson, Claudia, 12

Pearson, Gayle, 122
Pearson, Tracey Campbell, 129
Petrosino, Tamara, 80
Pfeffer, Wendy, 80
Pittman, Helena Clare, 101
Pitzer, Susanna, 101
Pollack, Pam, 101
Porte, Barbara Ann, 133
Powell, Patricia Hruby, 38
Pryor, Bonnie, 113

Quattlebaum, Mary, 137

Radley, Gail, 25
Ransom, Candice, 134
Rappaport, Doreen, 101
Ratto, Linda Lee, 31
Regan-Blake, Connie, 109
Richardson, Sandy, 126
Riffel, June, 140
Ritter, John, 101
Robbins, Dan, 38
Roop, Connie, 144
Roop, Peter, 144
Rothstein, Gloria, 25

Sanders, Jo, 31
Sandford, Mary Ellyn, 39
Santucci, Barbara, 39
Sayre, April Pulley, 42
Schaer, Miriam, 102
Schanzer, Rosalyn, 134
Schmidt, Karen Lee, 102
Schnitzlein, Danny, 31
Schrecengost, Maity, 25
Schutzgruber, Barbara, 66
Schwartz, Joyce, 51
Seabrooke, Brenda, 26
Sedar, Scott, 137
Seuling, Barbara, 102
Shalant, Phyllis, 103
Shaw, Susan, 118
Shea, Pegi Dietz, 16
Shore, Diane, 31
Sims, Jane, 26, 110

Sims, Wayne, 26, 110
Singhalaka, Pattima, 144
Slate, Joseph, 51
Smith, Kimanne, 80
Smith, Robert Kimmel, 103
Soentpiet, Chris, 103
Spirn, Michele Sobel, 103
Spitzer, Linda, 26
Sprengnether, Lois, 66
Springer, Nancy, 118
Stanley, Sanna, 17
Stavish, Corinne, 67
Stemple, Heidi Elisabet Yolen, 60
Steptoe, Javaka, 104
Stern, Ellen Norman, 119
Stivender, Ed, 119
Stock, Catherine, 104
Stockdale, Susan, 32
Stoutland, Allison, 67
Stroud, Bettye, 32
Sullivan, George, 104
Sutton, Jane, 61
Swallow, Pamela Curtis, 80
Sweet, Frank, 26
Sweet, Mary Lee, 26
Swope, Sam, 105

Tagliaferro, Linda, 105
Tamar, Erika, 105
Tarpley, Natasha, 106
Thompson, Julie, 72
Thompson, Melodie, 122
Thomson, Peggy, 51
Thomson, Ryan, 73
Tocher, Timothy, 106
Toledo, Tony, 61
Tomasello, Heather, 134
Trice, Linda, 27

Valance, Marsha, 144
Vanadia, David, 106
Vande Veld, Vivian, 106
Verniero, Joan, 17
Vernon, Learnin', 47
Vuranch, Karen, 140

Wahl, Jan, 113
Weiner, Marcella Bakur, 106
Weiss, Jim, 135
Welling, Peter, 42
Wells, Megan, 39
Wendt, Karen, 144
Weston, Carol, 107
Whalen, Erin, 122
Whitesel, Cheryl Aylward, 39
Whitman, Sylvia, 27
Wieder, Joy Nelkin, 61
Williams, Michael "Badhair", 110
Williams, Sylvia, 69
Winship, Jim, 145
Winston, David Lorenz, 119
Winters, Kay, 119
Winthrop, Elizabeth, 107
Wojciechowski, Susan, 120
Wolfman, Judy, 120
Wolkstein, Diane, 107
Wright, Lynn Floyd, 126
Wright, Susan Kimmel, 120

Yezerski, Thomas, 81
Yolen, Jane, 61

Zalben, Jane Breskin, 107
Zimmer, Melanie, 108
Zucker, Joyce, 108
Zucker, Naomi Flink, 123

Index by State

Alabama

Broerman, Joan, 11
Ghigna, Charles, 11
Kittinger, Jo, 11
Pearson, Claudia, 12

Connecticut

Abbott, Tony, 13
Barchers, Suzanne, 13
Baskin, Nora Raleigh, 13
Birch, Carol, 14
Fraustino, Lisa Rowe, 14
Gibson, Drew, 14
Himmelman, John, 15
Hubbell, Patricia, 15
Kudlinski, Kathleen, 15
Ladd, Louise, 15
Maestro, Betsy, 16
Maestro, Giulio, 16
Miller, Bobbi, 16
Shea, Pegi Dietz, 16
Stanley, Sanna, 17
Verniero, Joan, 17

Delaware

Kennedy, Mary, 19

Florida

Bea, Holly, 21
Berkes, Marianne, 21
Davis, Myra, 21
Derby, Ken, 22
Farnsworth, Bill, 22
Feeney, Kathy, 22
Freeman, Marcia, 22
Gail, Judy, 23
Gay, Kathlyn, 23
Hathaway, Lucinda, 23
Hausman, Gerald, 24
Kay, Alan, 24
Landau, Elaine, 24
Marcello, Patricia Cronin, 24
Martia, Dominic, 25
NeSmith, Phyllis, 21
Radley, Gail, 25
Rothstein, Gloria, 25
Schrecengost, Maity, 25
Seabrooke, Brenda, 26
Sims, Wayne, 26
Sims, Jane, 26
Spitzer, Linda, 26
Sweet, Frank, 26
Sweet, Mary Lee, 26
Trice, Linda, 27
Whitman, Sylvia, 27

Georgia

Chappas, Bess, 29
Cruzan, Patricia, 29
Karwoski, Gail Lerner, 29
Larkin, Chuck, 30
Myers, Laurie, 30
Mueller, Pamela Bauer, 30
Norfolk, Sherry, 30
Ratto, Linda Lee, 31
Sanders, Jo, 31
Schnitzlein, Danny, 31
Shore, Diane, 31
Stockdale, Susan, 32
Stroud, Bettye, 32

Illinois

Anderson, Mike, 33
Anzalotti, Pamela, 33
Billingsley, Franny, 33
Brill, Marlene Targ, 34
Burns, Phyllis Ann, 34
Collins, David, 34
Crimi, Carolyn, 34
Dague, James, 35
Ellis, Brian "Fox", 35
Fradin, Judith Bloom, 35
Gibson, Kathleen, 35
Gorham, Linda, 36
Gryniewicz, Gene, 36
Johnson-Webb, Anna, 36
Johnson, Leanne, 36
Kemba, Momma, 36
Kinsella, Marilyn, 37
Kummer, Patricia, 37
Luthardt, Kevin, 37
Lynn, Paddy, 37
Mallen, Lisa, 37
Miller, Maryjane, 38
Powell, Patricia Hruby, 38
Robbins, Dan, 38
Sandford, Mary Ellyn, 39
Santucci, Barbara, 39
Wells, Megan, 39
Whitesel, Cheryl Aylward, 39

Indiana

Clifton, Sharon Kirk, 41
Fincken, Hank, 41
Frost, Helen, 41
Kichler, Florrie Binford, 42
Marston, Elsa, 42
Sayre, April Pulley, 42
Welling, Peter, 42

Kentucky

Brown, Roberta Simpson, 43
Jones, Marcia Thornton, 43
Mora, Pat, 43

Maine

Baldwin, Robert, 45
Buzzeo, Toni, 45
Davidson, Robert, 45
Jacobson, Jennifer Richard, 46
Lint, David, 46
Dafydd the Storyteller, 46
Lovejoy, Sharon, 46
MacDonald, Amy, 46
McMillan, Bruce, 47
Packie, Tammy, 47
Vernon, Learnin', 47

Maryland

Bowen, Fred, 49
Butts, Ellen, 49
Cummings, Priscilla, 49
Faine, Edward Allen, 50
Golembe, Carla, 50
Green, Michelle, 50
Meacham, Margaret, 51
Schwartz, Joyce, 51
Slate, Joseph, 51
Thomson, Peggy, 51

Massachusetts

Beatty, Monica Driscoll, 53
Black, Judith, 53
Blatchford, Claire, 54
Collins, Pat Lowery, 54
Davies, Jacqueline, 54
Davol, Marguerite, 54
Dooley, Norah, 55
Finkelstein, Norman, 55
Francis, Michael, 55
Gantos, Jack, 55
Garden, Nancy, 56
Glaser, Michael, 56
Goldman, Dara, 56
Gormley, Beatrice, 57
Greenburg, Bonnie, 57
Jango-Cohen, Judith, 57
Juster, Norton, 57
Koller, Jackie French, 58
Krensky, Stephen, 58
Lessem, Don, 58
Leventhal, Rona, 59
Lies, Brian, 59
Lipke, Barbara, 59
McCabe, Tom, 59
Moffatt, Judith, 60
O'Connor, Barbara, 60
Pearl, Sydelle, 60
Stemple, Heidi Elisabet Yolen, 60
Sutton, Jane, 61
Toledo, Tony, 61
Wieder, Joy Nelkin, 61
Yolen, Jane, 61

Michigan

Appleton, Betty, 63
Bogar, Tim, 63
Bolley, Jean, 63
Dick, Linda, 63
Dodge, Christopher Jay, 64
Donlon, Diane Youngblood, 64
Ellis, Sid "The Rock", 64
Elster, Jean Alicia, 64
Greene, Rhonda Gowler, 64
Hansen, Sandra, 65
Healy, Yvonne, 65
Kammeraad, Kevin, 65
Luke, Linda, 65
Neitzel, Shirley, 66
Nelson, Ann Gieseler Bryan, 66
Schutzgruber, Barbara, 66
Sprengnether, Lois, 66
Stavish, Corinne, 67
Stoutland, Allison, 67

Mississippi

Williams, Sylvia, 69

New Hampshire

Allen, Mary Emma, 71
Bodkin, Odds, 71
Demarest, Chris, 71
Fletcher, Ralph, 72
Kenyon, Ross, 72
Klingler, Angela Cay, 72
Macintosh, Brownie, 72
Thompson, Julie, 72
Thomson, Ryan, 73

New Jersey

Adlerman, Danny, 75
Adlerman, Kim, 75
Eagle, Kin, 75
Brisson, Pat, 75
Cuyler, Margery, 76
Dooling, Michael, 76
Gutman, Dan, 76
Hirschfelder, Arlene, 76
Huling, Jan, 77
Huling, Phil, 77
Kaighn, Laura, 77
Karr, Susan Schott, 77
Kjelle, Marylou Moran, 77
Lanton, Sandy, 78
Lessac, Frané, 78
Lewis, E.B., 78
Macy, Sue, 79
Matero, Robert, 79
McDonald, Joyce, 79
Petrosino, Tamara, 80
Pfeffer, Wendy, 80
Smith, Kimanne, 80
Swallow, Pamela Curtis, 80
Yezerski, Thomas, 81

New York

Adler, David, 83
Alko, Selina, 83
Backtalk Productions, 87

Barkin, Carol, 83
Bart, Kathleen, 84
Beckhorn, Susan Williams, 84
Bellavia, Timothy, 84
Belviso, Meg, 101
Bradbury, Judy, 84
Brewster, Patience, 85
Brody, Janis, 85
Bruchac, James, 85
Bruchac, Joseph, 85
Calmenson, Stephanie, 86
Capucilli, Alyssa Satin, 86
Caseley, Judith, 86
Choi, Yangsook, 87
Clayson, Jill, 87
Cleary, Rita, 87
Clements, Jehan, 87
Cobb, Vicki, 88
Cohen, Caron Lee, 88
Collier, James Lincoln, 88
Corey, Shana, 88
Crompton, Laurie Ann, 89
Cusack, Margaret, 89
Czarnota, Lorna McDonald, 89
Daniels, Teri, 89
Davis, Gibbs, 90
Davis, Katie, 91
DeSpain, Pleasant, 90
Dubisch, Carolyn Watson, 90
Einhorn, Edward, 90
Feder, Harriet, 91
Feeney, Betsy Franco, 91
Foland, Constance, 91
Furstinger, Nancy, 92
Greenberg, Melanie Hope, 92
Greenburg, Dan, 92
Greenburg, Judith 92
Greenstein, Elaine, 93
Hall, Elizabeth, 93
Haskins, Jim, 93
Heusler, Marianna, 94
Holm, Jennifer, 94
Hurwitz, Johanna, 94
Intrater, Roberta Grobel, 94

Janovitz, Marilyn, 95
Jocelyn, Marthe, 95
Katz, Bobbi, 95
Kilborne, Sarah, 95
Korman, Gordon, 96
Kroll, Steven, 96
Land, Karen, 96
Lanza, Barbara, 96
Levinson, Marilyn, 97
Livingstone, Star, 97
Marston, Hope Irvin, 97
Marx, Trish, 97
Masoff, Joy, 98
Masters, Susan Rowan, 98
Mazer, Anne, 98
McGovern, Ann, 98
Miller, Genia, 87
Morse, Andy, 99
Munro, Roxie, 99
Newman, Aline Alexander, 99
Nobisso, Josephine "Joi", 99
Nobleman, Marc Tyler, 100
Noonan, Julia, 100
Park, Linda Sue, 100
Pittman, Helena Clare, 101
Pitzer, Susanna, 101
Pollack, Pam, 101
Rappaport, Doreen, 101
Ritter, John, 101
Schaer, Miriam, 102
Schmidt, Karen Lee, 102
Seuling, Barbara, 102
Shalant, Phyllis, 103
Smith, Robert Kimmel, 103
Soentpiet, Chris, 103
Spirn, Michele Sobel, 103
Steptoe, Javaka, 104
Stock, Catherine, 104
Sullivan, George, 104
Swope, Sam, 105
Tagliaferro, Linda, 105
Tamar, Erika, 105
Tarpley, Natasha, 106
Tocher, Timothy, 106
Vanadia, David, 106

Vande Veld, Vivian, 106
Weiner, Marcella Bakur, 106
Weston, Carol, 107
Winthrop, Elizabeth, 107
Wolkstein, Diane, 107
Zalben, Jane Breskin, 107
Zimmer, Melanie, 108
Zucker, Joyce, 108

North Carolina

Davis, Frances, 109
Jones, Ron, 109
Moore, MariJo, 109
Regan-Blake, Connie, 109
Sims, Jane, 110
Sims, Wayne, 110
Williams, Michael "Badhair", 110

Ohio

Alder, Elizabeth, 111
Ball, Liz, 111
Carson, Rick, 111
Cleary, Brian, 112
Mackall, Dandi Daley, 112
Miller, Brandon Marie, 112
Miller, Candace, 113
Pryor, Bonnie, 113
Wahl, Jan, 113

Pennsylvania

Baumgartner, Barbara, 115
Buchanan, Jane, 115
Donahue, Shari Faden, 115
Gorog, Judith, 116
High, Linda Oatman, 116
Howard, Elizabeth, Fitzgerald, 116
Keehn, Sally, 117
Lalli, Judy, 117
Long, Kathy, 117
Lubar, David, 117
Moore, Robin, 118

O'Connell, Rebecca, 118
Shaw, Susan, 118
Springer, Nancy, 118
Stern, Ellen Norman, 119
Stivender, Ed, 119
Wojciechowski, Susan, 120
Winston, David Lorenz, 119
Winters, Kay, 119
Wolfman, Judy, 120
Wright, Susan Kimmel, 120

Rhode Island

Brennan, Linda Crotta, 121
Cabral, Len, 121
Levitt, Marc Joel, 121
Parker, Barbara Keevil, 122
Pearson, Gayle, 122
Thompson, Melodie, 122
Whalen, Erin, 122
Zucker, Naomi Flink, 123

South Carolina

Fehler, Gene, 125
Hawkins, Suzette, 125
Johnson, Dinah, 125
Richardson, Sandy, 126
Wright, Lynn Floyd, 126

Tennessee

Barrett, Tracy, 127
Gove, Doris, 127
McIntyre, Karen, 127

Vermont

Beller, Susan Provost, 129
Pearson, Tracey Campbell, 129

Virginia

Bobrow, Laura, 131
Branch, Muriel Miller, 131
Campbell, Meredith, 131
Clarke, Ginjer, 132
Edwards, Pamela Duncan, 132
Goodman, Linda, 132
Jules, Jacqueline, 132
Leotta, Joan, 133
May, Kathy, 133
Moore, Elaine, 133
Porte, Barbara Ann, 133
Ransom, Candice, 134
Schanzer, Rosalyn, 134
Tomasello, Heather, 134
Weiss, Jim, 135

Washington, D.C.

Quattlebaum, Mary, 137
Sedar, Scott, 137

West Virginia

Dadisman, Jo Ann, 139
Donovan, Connie, 139
Fraenkel, Andy, 139
Hairston, Bill, 139
Holstein, Susanna "Granny Sue", 140
Riffel, June, 140
Vuranch, Karen, 140

Wisconsin

Addy, Sharon Hart, 141
Burns, Diane, 141
Dickman, Jean-Andrew, 141
Garrison, R. Hardy, 142
Ivanko, John, 142
Jensen, Bob, 142
Jensen, Janet, 142
Kann, Bob, 143

Laundrie, Amy, 143
Lorbiecki, Marybeth, 143
Macken, JoAnn Early, 143
Roop, Connie, 144
Roop, Peter, 144
Singhalaka, Pattima, 144
Valance, Marsha, 144
Wendt, Karen, 144
Winship, Jim, 145

About the Author

Gwynne Spencer has always loved children's books best. When she was a teacher, she depended on real, live books, not textbooks, to teach beginning reading, remedial skills, and everything in between. When she was a bookstore owner, she sponsored many author events, both in her store and in schools; set up collaborations between the bookstore and public libraries; and organized writers' conferences and storytelling events to help connect talented folks to eager audiences.

She has also written the book *What's Cooking in Children's Literature* (Linworth, 2001) and *Recipes for Reading* (Linworth, 2002), as well as hundreds of columns and articles about children's books for newspapers and magazines. She also teaches courses on story structure, memoir writing, and children's literature at various writers' conferences, nationwide. Contact her at *pengwynnes@aol.com*.

www.ingramcontent.com/pod-product-compliance
Lightning Source LLC
Chambersburg PA
CBHW080540300426